Best wishes a

Life in the Skillet

—and lessons learned along the way—

Harold D. Fanning

Dedication

This book is dedicated to my two granddaughters, Audrey and Anna, who are teaching me more about the wonders of life than I'll ever teach them.

Foreword

Whoever said, "Some people tell funny stories, while others tell stories funny," must have known Harold Fanning! For a number of years I have been reading his pastor's column in the monthly church newsletter with great joy and delight. Many church bulletins I receive are cast aside with just a casual glance—but not his! I am seldom disappointed when I read his articles.

Harold Fanning has a unique and charming way of sharing actual everyday events, seeing the humorous side of them, and then carefully weaving into the story clear and helpful spiritual applications. He is a master storyteller!

For a number of years I have repeatedly encouraged him to consider putting some of those monthly columns into book form so that they may have a much wider circulation. I am genuinely elated that he has now chosen to do that. I predict that these brief chapters will leave the reader both tickled and blessed—and waiting for even more!

Evangelist Junior Hill
Hartselle, Alabama

Prologue

"O ye simple, understand wisdom: and, ye fools, be ye of
an understanding heart."
Proverbs 8:5

Growing up in Lick Skillet, Alabama, during the time that my sisters and I were in grammar school was, for the most part, a simple life. There wasn't much television watched in those days. As a matter of fact, for years the only television set within a twenty-five mile radius of our house belonged to my grandparents. Watching that old black and white Philco that my grandfather had purchased at a local Montgomery Wards department store often proved to be more entertainment than the shows themselves. I suppose that the word "reception" was a foreign concept to television manufacturers back then because most of the time what you saw on the screen was more like looking at figures through a winter snowstorm. Any attempt to adjust the reception usually required one of my uncles standing outside next to the antenna—which was mounted on a pole about twenty feet above the roof line—with all of us yelling across the room through an open window our contrasting instructions on which way he needed to turn the thing.

Sometimes the best reception was gained when one of us simply laid our hand on the antenna pole itself. We always hated that, especially if my grandfather happened to be watching professional wrestling. That meant the entire family would have to take turns holding the antenna pole so he could see the screen clearly. He would get so wrapped up in watching the Masked Marauder, Nut House Fargo and Dusty Rhodes that he would literally fight, flop, and flip the chair he was sitting in. He would yell and scream at that television set if his favorite wrestler happened to be losing the round. To be honest, my dad used to say that the best show was watching my grandfather watch wrestling.

Life in Lick Skillet was eventful to say the least. Unlike some of the town meetings, support for our beloved LSU (Lick Skillet University as we called it. Actually, it was New Sharon Middle School, but it was always referred to by the locals as LSU) sporting events were an opportunity for the entire community to find some semblance of commonality among its residents.

Back then there was no such thing as a grandstand therefore everyone had to sit on sawmill run, rough-cut oak boards that were constructed and paid for by the PTA and the LSU alumni association. Automobiles could be driven up pretty close to the base lines and most people (especially the women) would simply sit in the car and knit and occasionally yell at their kids. Every now and then when someone would make a good play and excite the crowd they might look up from what they were doing just to see what was going on. Most people simply walked around with their popcorn, hotdogs, and soft drinks visiting with each other talking local politics, religion, the farm situation, or how unusually hot the weather was that year.

Winter days usually meant visiting relatives on Sunday afternoon, and for us that meant another trip to my grandparents' house. Spending time in a crowded house with a television that had bad reception was always eventful. My mother had seven siblings who usually showed up along with their own immediate families. You can only imagine what it was like to be crammed into a 1,500 square-foot house with all those in-laws, grandchildren, invited neighbors, fellow churchgoers, etc. For us kids we usually drew pictures, picked at each other, played cards and board games while the adults talked about everything from how cold it was to the political processes and what a mess the Republicans had gotten us into. More times than not, being cooped up in that house with all those cousins would eventually prove too much and we would end up in a big fight, usually resulting in us taking sides against each other.

The community of Lick Skillet wasn't much different from any other Southern town. Life was simple, the people worked hard, most attended church and all were involved in one way or the other in local activities. Farming was a way of life with cotton, corn, soybeans, and wheat being the major crops produced. Lick Skillet also had its share of small general stores, seemingly situated everywhere. There was no need to travel to the larger towns like Huntsville or Fayetteville because you could usually get anything you needed right there in the Skillet. Commodities like gasoline, kerosene, food items, pocket knifes, farming supplies, and everything from hand grenades to Gatlin guns were available.

Growing up in the Skillet is what this book is all about. The reader should be cautioned not to be too hasty in simply assuming that this is merely a collection of childhood stories written by a middle-aged man reminiscing about old times. I'm sure if my neighbors living in the Skillet during this same time period were asked, their memories of these same events would be radically different... I just tend to have a more unique perspective than most folks! The reader should also be aware that the names found on these pages have been changed to protect the guilty! While some of the incidents written about here have been a bit exaggerated, the reader can be assured that they are all based on true events. But these stories go much farther and have much more to say than merely stirring your childhood memories of days gone by. This is not just a simple gathering of humorous stories about the past, but rather a gathering of lessons learned that literally shaped my own philosophies and ideas about life.

We are living in a society that has, for the most part, forgotten what community is all about. Many of us, if we would be honest, do not know (nor do we care) who our neighbors are anymore. Modern America has become so accustomed to the use of the Internet that we have virtually cut our association (or our need) to be with other people. We can shop, communicate, travel the world, and search for a custom-made spouse. We can order a new automobile and look at a new house without actually leaving the comfort of our homes or the companionship of our computers. I feel this is sad and we have an entire generation that will never understand the meaning of what community truly is.

The tragedy of all this is the fact that we are missing the whole reason why we were created to begin with. I do not know if you realize it, but the bottom-line reason God made mankind was for fellowship and community. God's desire is that we have a personal relationship with Him through His Son, Jesus Christ, which in turn ultimately results in a positive relationship with others. The purpose of the creation, the purpose of the cross of Christ, and the purpose of the church is so we can experience the true meaning of *community,* which will one day be eternally realized in heaven.

This book is the result of the encouragement and input of many different people. I want to thank...

...My wife, Deborah, for always being there with her valuable advice and constant love.

...My daughter, Alison Creel, for editing and proofing the manuscript many times.

...My son, Daniel Fanning, for encouraging me to write these stories.

...My friend, Dr. Junior Hill, for his continued encouragement and for writing the foreword to this work for me.

...To the wonderful people of Lick Skillet who are some of the greatest neighbors and friends anyone could ever have.

The Barn Swing

"Happy is the man that findeth wisdom, and the man that
getteth understanding."
Proverbs 3:13

Life in the Skillet in the late 50s and early 60s was sometimes difficult. The winters were cold, the summers
were hot, and the work hard. For a group of ten-year-old
boys it also meant making the most out of what you had, or
in some cases, what you found. Such was the case in the
summer of 1962 when some of my childhood friends and I
discovered an old, discarded electrical cord.

Please allow me to explain! Finding something as great as
a twenty-foot electrical cord swings the door of opportunity
wide open to all kinds of interesting and innovative possibili-
ties. Immediately, all our creative mental wheels began spin-
ning as to what we could do with such a prize find.

Hence, after much discussion, we finally agreed on a
plan of taking that old cord and constructing a really neat
swing in the barn loft. With our discarded twenty-foot electrical cord, a twelve-inch hickory stick, and a pair of Globe
Master wire pliers we made our way to the barn. Our intentions were to tie one end of the cord around one of the barn

rafters and position it so that when you made your initial launch off a stack of hay bales you would travel forward, then upward and *out* the loft entrance (which was about twenty feet from the ground) and then return to the bale of hay from where you started. The design was nothing short of genius and the plan brilliant.

So, with the best of intentions, we took the cord and the hickory stick (which would eventually be used for the seat) and ascended the ladder leading to the loft. After securing our contraption to a rafter we were ready for action. We swung all morning on that electrical cord, enjoying every blissful moment until the unthinkable happened.

Just before lunch, in one fatal swoop, we learned a valuable lesson in physics as well as confirmed Sir Isaac Newton's theory of gravity. Unbeknownst to us, we had overlooked one, small detail. For you see, every time that swing went back and forth, the copper wires in that cord were getting hotter and hotter and weaker and weaker. And sadly, I happened to be the one to which the laws of physics unmercifully bestowed their full wrath and fury. For just as I made that one last upward swing (with a tomato sandwich and a RC cola on my mind for lunch) the wires broke and launched me forward like a paper wad from a rubber band. The first thing that hit the ground was my backside and the next was my head. After that all I remember were my friends and family with a corn scoop doing their best to dislodge what was left of my broken body from the crater that I had created approximately thirty yards from the front of that barn (a slight exaggeration). It was in the midst of my misery that I realized a very valuable biblical truth that would ultimately aid me in my ministerial theological training years later, *"From dust you came and to dust you will return."* It was also somewhere about this time that my dear old daddy made a profound statement that I've never forgotten: "I could have told you fellas that would happen!" Gee, thanks, Dad.

Isn't it interesting how some of our most valuable lessons are learned in the pit of pain? We start off with the best of intentions but somewhere along the line something happens that causes the whole thing to unravel. Either it is something we've overlooked or someone interferes.

Did you know that God uses the sandpaper of our mistakes and the mistakes of others to grow and mature us? I'm convinced that God intentionally allows people into our lives who have obvious personality faults just to humble us. Those people who seem to have more than their abundance of impatience, meanness, laziness, irresponsibility, and inconsideration can be tools in the hands of God. These people can irritate, frustrate, and generally ruin an otherwise nice day.

But you want to know something interesting? While we are longing and praying and begging for God to change them, the fact is, we discover that He's trying to change us! It is at this point when we realize (sometimes too late) that all those personality traits we hate in others are also true of us. We need to understand that many times when we hit the bottom (or on your bottom) it is more often than not a ride of our own making. Usually it is something we've failed to understand or something simple we've overlooked.

Believe me; I learned some valuable lessons on that swing that day. I learned that your friends laugh at you when you fall down. I learned that Alabama dirt makes an RC Cola taste like a Yoo-hoo. And probably more importantly, I learned that sometimes your father's philosophical meanderings ought to be kept to himself! But am I bitter? Who me? Nooooo... I just can't seem to remember the names of those friends! But I forgive them!

Winners and Losers

"A false balance is abomination to the Lord:
but a just weight is his delight."
Proverbs 11:1

Have you ever pondered what a winner is? What about a loser? What is your opinion of what defines a winner or loser?

When I was a senior in high school we voted on *Who's Who* for the annual high school yearbook. The student body would evaluate their classmates and decide among their peers who was the smartest (I didn't get that one); the best looking (I placed but didn't win that one either); most popular, etc. One of those categories was *"Most Likely to Succeed."* I don't mind admitting that even as a high school student I had problems with that one. For me personally, I just never understood the criteria for making such a judgment. Are we talking about potential income, athletic abilities, physical features, public opinions, popular trends, or what? How do you evaluate who is most likely to succeed or who will end up being the winner in life?

Actually, this is one of those statements that have both a positive and a negative response. For example, in my opinion, winning or losing is summarized by how you view both issues. It is my belief that coming in first is one of the finest things one can do. Why? Because everybody loves a winner, that's why! Have you ever noticed that a sports team, whether it is high school, college, or professional, usually has virtually no fans as long as they are losing? But let the team start winning every game with the possibility of a state or national championship and you cannot find a seat in the house. The fans will wear the jerseys, purchase the caps and cups, and proudly display the bumper stickers. Why? Because people have a natural bent toward winning and a desire to associate with winners!

Don't let me raise your blood pressure! This is nothing to be ashamed of. We just need to get down to where the rubber meets the road and confess that we like to win. After all, no one really remembers who finished second, right? Do you remember who came in second at the Indy 500 last year? I know the winner was a virtual unknown who seemingly came out of nowhere and literally smoked the entire field. But for the life of me I cannot remember who came in second!

Winning enables us to fulfill our personal goals; it gives us a feeling of accomplishment. Winning means that all the factors came together and on this day we were the best in our field. There is nothing wrong with that. We all need to feel we are a part of something great!

But what if we lose? Now that is a different ballgame. Actually, it all depends upon your definition of losing. Coming in second, third, or even dead last does not necessarily mean that we are a loser. When we lose while attempting something grand, we actually end up winning. Oh, we may not get the trophy, blue ribbon, or the press coverage, but when the lessons learned by losing are used as stepping stones to something greater, losing transforms into winning.

Thoroughly confused? Let me see if I can clarify a bit. When I was fourteen years old some friends and I decided we would spend the weekend camping next to a pond located behind our house. The pond was owned by a neighbor who gladly gave us permission to be on his property.

We laughed, played, and had a wonderful time being together and talking about things that fourteen-year-old boys generally talk about—usually fourteen-year-old girls!

Anyway, around 8:00 p.m. we were becoming hungry and one of us (I honestly do not remember who) suggested that we be real pioneers and cook frog legs over an open fire for dinner. So we found a stick about six feet long, tied an old butcher knife to one end and set about the task of "gigging" as many frogs as we could (sorry, but that is a common practice in the rural South). We gathered every frog we could find and cooked and ate frog legs until we were all nearly sick.

The next morning we woke up and decided we'd had about as much fun as we could stand and commenced to break camp. We cleaned everything as best we could and headed for home. Actually, I thought that was the end of it and did not give it much thought from that point on.

Monday was a school day, so my two sisters and I climbed aboard the bus, as was our regular routine. But on this occasion, the daughter of the landowner where we had camped asked me to sit next to her. When I sat down she informed me that her father was extremely upset and desperately wanted to speak with my dad and me. Panic-stricken, I immediately hit the rewind button of my mind trying to remember anything that we might have done wrong. I did not have to wait long before she explained to me that her father had purchased those frogs for the sole purpose of keeping the mosquito population under control. He had apparently gone down to his pond after we broke camp and had discovered the evidence of our great frog leg cook off and was very irritated. He was demanding accountability as well as restitution for his loss. As a fourteen-year-old boy I have to admit that I was frightened beyond belief and did not know what I was going to do. The thought of having to explain to this man what we had done nearly resulted in me becoming sick right there in front of everyone on that bus. And not only that, but I spent the entire day at school thinking about what I was going to say to him. I created some of the most unbelievable lies I could muster in my attempts to justify my actions.

Finally, school was out and I had to make that long journey home to face my accuser. When my dad finally arrived home from work I took the first step and told him what we had done. He immediately put me in the car and off to the neighbors we went. I prayed, "Oh God, please let us have a traffic accident or an alien space craft abduct us, or an elephant crush the car before we get there. Anything, please God, just anything!"

We pulled into our neighbor's driveway and I immediately spied him sitting in a chair under a giant oak tree. My dad and I walked over to him and the first words that were spoken came from my father, "Sam, Harold has something to say to you!" There I was. The time had come, the trap was set, the gig was up and I think the fat lady sang. I began explaining that we didn't know about his purchasing the frogs and how sorry I was and how I would be willing to work on his farm after school to repay any damages. As best I could I spilled my guts, groveled in the dirt, squirmed and twisted in my embarrassment. And I'm not sure, but between you and me, I think I even cried a little!

That is when my neighbor said something that I have never forgotten. He responded, "Harold, I sent word to every one of those boys that camped this past weekend that I wanted to talk to them. As of right now, you are the only one who has shown up. I also want you to know that I realize it took courage for you to come here today and I truly appreciate your offer to pay for any damages. But I want you to know something else, *your willingness to tell the truth and own up to your mistake is all the payment I need. As far as I am concerned this matter between you and me is a closed issue!"* You know something interesting? I found out later that not another one of my camping companions ever went to that neighbor to apologize. I'm not sure, but I am fairly confident that our neighbor's disappointment in my friends went with him to his grave. Today the only thing that remains of Sam's old home place is that huge oak tree under which he was sitting that day. For me that tree stands as a visual reminder of what forgiveness extended is all about.

Do you understand the moral of this story? A winner can come in second, third, or even last. Just the fact that you participated is a fantastic achievement and proves that you have the heart of a winner, no matter where you placed.

What about the majority who didn't bother to enter the race or attempt to make a wrong right? Have you ever noticed that losers usually sit around with other non-participants and gripe and complain about those who competed? Sadly, these are the real losers. Losers are those who never enter the race simply because they are afraid they will fail. A loser is someone who is found sitting instead of standing during a crisis. A loser looks for the negatives in everyone, everything, and every situation. Losers are takers, grumblers, complainers, and generally a leach on society and everyone else around them. Losers sit idly by and allow others to wait on them hand and foot and refuse to take the blame even though they are equally guilty. Losers are never going to accomplish anything positive and whine when someone else does. Losers look for an ulterior motive of the winner and wrongly assume they must have had an unfair advantage that gave them the edge.

Losers are those who will not vote during an election yet complain about the actions and decisions of elected officials. Losers take advantage of every government give-away program without contributing anything back. Losers fake physical injury so they can receive disability checks without working. Losers look for reasons to sue others in court over frivolous and exaggerated reasons. The list of what I feel describes a loser is never ending.

But before we end, there is a third group we need to address—the participants who entered but sought to win by questionable means. Somehow our society has bought the idea that they *deserve* the win, and the means by which it is obtained is okay.

When I was growing up in the 60s and 70s most parents taught their children that it was morally wrong to cheat, steal, or be untruthful. But somewhere along the way those ethical standards slowly began to erode and now many have convinced themselves that they can obtain the win by any means necessary.

Worse, we have also learned to justify our actions with philosophies like, "Everybody else is doing it, why can't I?" If this is our line of thinking then somewhere we've missed the entire concept of what winning and losing truly means. There is no excuse for "winning at all cost!" The end does not justify the means when the end is obtained by questionable and dishonest methods. We cannot claim the crown if the victory was won by dubious tactics. Where is the honor when the trophy sitting on your shelf or the gold metal hanging around your neck was won by questionable and underhanded means? Wouldn't you agree that preserving truth and honesty is just as important as the actual win? And greater still, if you work to preserve truth, justice, and righteousness, when your character is on the line or your motives are questioned you will never have to remember who you cheated or to whom you lied or stole from.

The apostle Paul writing to the Corinthian church said, "We have wronged no man, we have corrupted no man, we have defrauded no man" (2 Corinthians 7:2 KJV). Wow, what a statement! This may not seem like a big deal now but one day what others say about you at your funeral will be important! You may respond, "I'll be dead so why should I care what people will say?" Because your life is a legacy and all of us are currently making a historical statement. Yes, you may be dead but your influences, philosophies, the way you treated others—both positive and negative—will affect your friends and family for generations.

What will they say about you? Will they testify of your honesty and how your words were your bond? Will there be people in attendance who you assisted in difficult situations?

Or will they bury you in a coffin that was purchased with funds gained by questionable means? Will there be those in attendance who will be relieved to see you go? Will there be people you defrauded at your funeral, people to whom you owe debts they will never recover? Will they testify that you are an honest and upright person? So what is your true definition of a winner?

A Hard Lesson in Humiliation

"As cold waters to a thirsty soul,
so is good news from a far country."
Proverbs 25:25

Have you ever been so humiliated that you wanted to die and simply evaporate into oblivion? Or maybe you have pondered being like one of those guys who tells his wife he is going to the store to purchase milk and bread and is never heard from again. Or what about those people who fake their death, only to be discovered fifty years later living in California where they have served as governor or something?

I have never done anything like that, but there was an incident in my life that certainly warranted my trying to pull off such a stunt!

It started on a Monday morning when I was in the fifth grade at LSU (Lick Skillet University). For some reason I had overslept and in my haste I grabbed the first white shirt I saw, put it on and headed off to school. To make matters worse, I didn't realize what I had done until we went out on the baseball field during third period physical education class. It was on that baseball field that one of my (supposed) friends finally told me what all the pointing, laughing, and snickering was about. I could hardly believe it! There I was, waiting to be chosen for a team, wearing the prettiest little girlie blouse known to man. It was complete with a rounded collar, cute blue flowers, trimmed lace, and heart-shaped buttons down the front. It was then that I realized the grave error – I had mistakenly picked up my sister's white blouse assuming it was one of my shirts.

In my disgrace and desperation I searched and finally found an old leather motorcycle jacket someone had abandoned the previous winter, so I put it on to help cover my shame. After school I walked almost three miles home enduring 100-degree heat wearing my sister's blouse and a leather motorcycle jacket! Furthermore, I don't know if you believe this, but are you aware that most people will not pick up a hitchhiker dressed in a blouse and leather motorcycle jacket?

And not only that, but some people you have known all your life will drive right past you and never wave nor acknowledge your presence. Then there are others you thought were your friends and neighbors - good Christian Americans who attend church, drive Chevrolets, and eat apple pie that will whistle at you and mockingly ask for a date and send flowers.

What's the moral of this? Are you kidding? Here you are reading this story thinking nobody has problems like yours? You need to be reminded that we all have problems, some just happen to be bigger than others. But what we need to understand is that our difficulties are not necessarily bad. Often they are instruments in the hand of God to aid our personal growth and maturity. Enduring the difficult circumstances of life helps us appreciate those wonderful days when the pressure is off and our blood pressure is somewhat normal.

Don't get me wrong! Problems aren't something I go out and look for, but let's face it, we all encounter them at some time or another. And, despite our best efforts, life just happens. All it takes is one phone call, one misspoken word, one bad decision, one *anything* and you can find yourself smack in the middle of a problem.

So, maybe you didn't wear your sister's blouse to school, but if nothing else, this story ought to help you really appreciate Proverbs 25:25, "As cold waters to a thirsty soul, so is good news from a far country." I don't know about you, but when you have had a day like mine that *far country* part sounds pretty good!

Showroom Slip-up

"He that diligently seeketh good procureth favour: but he
that seeketh mischief, it shall come unto him."
Proverbs 11:27

D id you know that jumping to hasty conclusions can be
very costly, in more ways than one? This fact is illustrated by a true incident that happened to one of my good
friends several years ago. Not willing to make monthly
payments, my friend had been working two jobs plus accu-
mulating all the overtime he could to purchase the automobile of his dreams: a brand new Cadillac Coupe DeVille.
For months all he talked about was his excitement and
anticipation of when the new models would arrive in show-
rooms and how he planned to purchase the first one. He
even had pictures he had cut from an automotive magazine
and had them posted proudly over his workstation for
everyone to see.

Finally the day arrived when all his hard work and
personal discipline paid off and he had enough funds saved
to make a cash purchase. He was so excited and could
hardly sleep the night before. His wife shared with me that
the next morning he was out of bed, showered, and dressed

before dawn and was sitting at the dealership before any of the sales personnel arrived. He had the money in the bank and a clear picture in his head of what he wanted, so he proudly walked into that Cadillac showroom determined to have his dreams and hard work become a reality.

But there was a slight problem that my friend soon discovered that ultimately proved to detour his plan. See, he was an African-American, middle-aged family man who had a quiet demeanor and a very big heart. He consistently wore a ball cap and jeans, worked hard, and always did his job with no complaints. Unless you had intentionally noticed him he was one of those individuals you never realized was in the room, he just simply blended in with the crowd. All these combined factors would create an interesting scenario that would eventually manifest itself in a unique way.

Finally, the dealership opened for business and he hurried into the showroom. The salesmen ignored him as they were busy talking with each other about the weekend college football games. Other than an occasional glance now and then, for the most part, he was totally overlooked. My friend walked around the new cars in the showroom, casually glancing toward the salesmen, who in turn must have assumed he was just a guy with more dreams than money. Finally, just to be nice, one of the men came over and with some air of impatience inquired if he needed help. My friend replied, "Yep! I want to buy that new Coupe DeVille right over there," pointing in the direction of the new car. "Okay," replied the salesman as he opened the car door for my friend to take a better look. But as my buddy was sitting in the car, the salesman made a big mistake by asking a simple question, "Do you think you can afford this car?" That question my friend never answered—he just got out of the car and quietly walked out of that showroom.

And walk he did—to the Lincoln Mercury dealer and purchased a brand-new Lincoln Continental Mark VIII for the cash sum of $42,000. But before he drove his new car home he made a quick detour to that Cadillac dealership. He parked at the front door, went inside and requested to see the salesman he had spoken with earlier that morning. He led him outside and showed him his new Lincoln as well as his *paid in full* papers. Furthermore, as he was getting behind the wheel to leave, he simply and quietly stated, "And to answer your question, yes sir, I can afford this car!"

Hopefully, that dumbfounded salesman learned a valuable lesson that day. See, he made the common but costly mistake of stereotyping others based solely on their appearance. This is the reason Jesus said, "Judge not, that ye be not judged" (Matthew 7:1 KJV). Also, speaking to the religious leaders, Jesus said, "Even so ye also outwardly appear righteous unto men, but within ye are full of hypocrisy and iniquity" (Matthew 23:28 KJV).

Someone has rightly said, "You can't judge a book by its cover." This principle also applies in our personal evaluations and hasty judgments of others when we solely base our opinions on outward appearances. Our salesman forgot one little bitty bit of information that he simply overlooked—my friend's skin was black but his money was green! Even more importantly, he also forgot the fact that my friend was a human being! Making hasty judgments can be very costly in more ways than one! Think about it!

A Bike, a Black Racer, and a Bad Decision!

"Go not forth hastily to strive,
lest thou know not what to do in the end thereof,
when thy neighbor hath put thee to shame."
Proverbs 25: 8

My dad passed away in the winter of 1999 after a battle with cancer. Shortly before his death, he and I were sitting on the rear porch of his house and he shared with me a humorous story that involved him and one of his cousins.

It was the summer of 1941 when my dad's cousin arrived at his house for a visit. Their plans were to spend the entire day doing what twelve-year-olds do—getting into things they shouldn't! At the time my dad was the proud owner of an old worn out bicycle that someone had discarded at the dump. Thrilled over the find, he had pulled the old bicycle from the array of cans, glass bottles, and other disgusting items and proudly carried his prize back home so he could do the proper repairs. With a bit of elbow grease, baling wire, and some blue house paint he'd found in the barn, he had the old bike back in a somewhat rideable condition in no time. That is, with the exception of one small, minor detail: it had no brakes! Also, just for informational purposes, the house where my dad lived was situated on a high hill that had a long winding gravel driveway that made a sharp right turn at the bottom (this sharp turn is worth remembering). There were also ditches on both sides of the driveway, a result of years of rain and erosion.

Here we have two twelve-year-old boys, a hill, and a bicycle with no brakes! Does this sound like the proper ingredients to a melodrama or what?

Okay, here's the rest of the story. Without asking permission or at least getting some vital information, dad's cousin spied that pretty blue bicycle parked by the front porch. He immediately ran over to the bike, jumped on and started his descent down that long driveway. And before my dad could inform him about the brakes, he was well on his way down that steep driveway. All my dad could do was yell, "Hey, that bike doesn't have any brakes!" To which the cousin responded by pushing back on the pedals, thus proving that indeed there were no brakes!

This is where one bad decision based on a lack of information gets worse. About halfway down that gravel driveway, there happened to be the most beautiful, shiny black racer snake you have ever seen crossing the road. He was approximately four feet in length and was simply out for a stroll, minding his own business, probably searching for his daily supply of frogs, rats, and other delicacies. Talk about being in the wrong place at the wrong time! For just as he slithered all four feet of his shiny black body in the middle of that gravel driveway, dad's cousin ran over him. The speed, coupled with the mysterious elements of physics unknown to primitive man at the time, sucked that snake up into the front spokes of that speeding bicycle. Needless to say, dad's cousin was greatly concerned by now.

Think it can't get any worse? Not only did the snake get

wound up in the spokes of the front wheel, but thirty seconds later the force and speed of that wheel literally tossed that snake up and he landed squarely in the lap of dad's cousin.

Still think it can't get any worse? Remember the sharp turn at the bottom of that gravel driveway? Okay, this is where that part of the story fits in. Fighting and flailing at a snake that wants off the bicycle as badly as dad's cousin; it was about at this point that a serious decision had to be made. So, overwhelmed by his current circumstances and stresses, he made a grave error in judgment (other than getting on the bicycle in the first place) by figuring that his best option was to simply ride this storm to its dreadful and woeful climatic end. And end it did—when the bike got to that curve—Dad's cousin missed it! There was nothing but fraying legs, arms, bent metal, and a wounded snake for at least thirty minutes (personal estimation) after he missed that curve. The cousin lay bleeding, bruised, and battered, the bike went back to the trash heap from where it came, and no one to this day knows what became of the snake. But I'll tell you a secret; I wouldn't be surprised if that snake had one unbelievable story to tell his friends!

Are we going to get something biblical out of this? Of course! Proverbs 25:8 says, "Go not forth hastily to strive, lest thou know not what to do in the end thereof." I guess there is a lesson in all this somewhere. I suppose the best advice would be to make absolutely sure you get all your facts clearly understood before making a hasty decision. I can assure you that the old adage, "What you don't know can't hurt you" is a lie as well as a disaster waiting to happen. Don't believe me? Well then, why don't you just ask the snake?

Just Over the Horizon

"The liberal soul shall be made fat: and he that watereth
shall be watered also himself."
Proverbs 11:25

My first airplane ride was an unforgettable experience.
The plane was a Cessna 172 that had only enough
room in the front seats for two average-sized adults and a
back compartment just big enough for one of those "black
boxes." Honesty dictates that I admit the interior space
didn't make much difference to me because my bottom side
was drawn up so tightly that I probably could have fit
perfectly in the crack between the seats anyway!

I remember that little engine winding up and my watching the propeller whirling at what appeared to be only
inches from the tip of my toes. As we taxied to the end of
the runway the pilot turned the RPMs up on that little
Cessna engine to what seemed to me to be at least 20,000. I
was confident the RPMs had to be off the charts because the
propeller disappeared into nothing but a blur. Just before
take off the pilot locked the brakes and I could feel the
RPMs tugging on that plane as though it couldn't wait to get
down the runway and into the air. The noise was incredible

and at the precise moment I thought my eardrums would pop, the pilot released the brakes and that plane shot down the runway like a bullet out of a gun.

We hadn't gotten very far down the runway when the pilot said something that I found disturbing. He commented, "You know, I haven't flown this thing in about a year and I'm having to refamilarize myself with everything!"

You honestly do not want to know what went through my mind at that point. I can admit it wasn't very Christian and definitely not ministerial. I didn't say a bad word, but if I had spit on the ground the grass would have died! It was at that *exact* moment that I had a theological understanding of Matthew 28:20, "and LO I am with you always" (personal interpretation).

Have you ever been called upon to do something that you weren't sure you could do? Your self-confidence drops to zero, your heart begins to race, and you end up making excuses why that task would be a personal impossibility?

Experiencing doubts and fears is natural, but if we insist on allowing them to rule our life we are going to miss out on some great experiences. We need to get out of our comfort zone and explore new horizons. Try writing a book, starting a business, flying a plane. Or, if you are not that aggressive, take a walk, play a game, or visit a nursing home. Life is just too short to stay cooped up in our own little world. Remember, there are new horizons just waiting for you to take advantage of if you are willing to take the risk!

Following Instructions

"Hear counsel, and receive instruction, that thou mayest
be wise in thy latter end."
Proverbs 19:20

The year 1990 was the dreaded year when our daughter
turned fifteen and took the test for her driver's permit.
Unfortunately for me, she passed with flying colors, thus
obligating me to teach her how to drive a car. As soon as we
got home she immediately wanted the lessons to begin. I
reluctantly agreed and decided to start off slowly by showing her the workings of an automobile and explaining how
each part (like the steering wheel, accelerator, brake, turn
signals, etc.) worked together to create a harmonious
masterpiece we call driving.

She listened intently and I was convinced that I was
clear in my explanations and persuaded that she understood
precisely every detail. For personal assurance I decided to
begin with a short trip, only about two miles to the grammar
school, just to make sure. I'd drive first while she observed,
then I'd turn the wheel over to her for the trip home.

Have you ever had one of those days when you've done
all the ground work, explained all the details, worked out all

the kinks, and then simply have everything explode in your face? That was definitely the case with me and it turned out to be my daughter's first (and last) driving lesson with Dad. She started off fine, just a little wobble here and there. I thought she was doing okay, until we got to the driveway of our house.

Before I tell you what happened next you need a clear understanding that our driveway, approximately eight feet wide, crossed a deep ditch. Situated next to the driveway was our mailbox; about twenty feet behind the mailbox was a huge maple tree. To make a successful turn you had to almost completely stop then slooooooowly ease into the driveway.

Okay, here's what happened—my daughter was traveling at approximately 120 mph (actually it was more like 40 mph, but believe me it seemed like 120!). When she was about 100 feet from the turn I *calmly* instructed her to slowly press on the brake. Instead, she kept on traveling and was not slowing down one bit. By now I had decided she was simply going to proceed past the driveway and maybe turn around down the road somewhere. Think that is what happened? Oh n-o-o-o-o!

When her front tires got parallel with the driveway entrance she immediately made a hard right turn, resulting in our making at least six 360s across our front yard. Somehow, with luck and some divine intervention, that kid missed the mailbox, the maple tree, the neighbor's mobile home, and all my personal belongings that I hold dear (like my life). That little Dodge Lancer came to a stop on our property line resting next to the neighbor's house, all without a single scratch on us or the car! I'm telling you the truth when I say that a professional race car driver couldn't have made that turn!

When I finally got enough strength in my legs to get out of the car, I again calmly said to my teenage daughter, "What do you think you're doing? Didn't I explain what that little pedal on the floorboard is? It's called a brake!!" To which she responded by running into the house crying and upset and said to my wife, "Daddy yelled at me and I didn't do anything!" When I attempted to explain to my wife what really happened she said, "Don't you think you're exaggerating this just a little?" To which I responded, "Sure, I'm exaggerating! Tell you what, I'll call an exaggerated wrecker service to get the car back to the exaggerated driveway, and you teach her how to drive!" Of course all of this was done calmly!

Have you ever wondered why God puts up with us? Isn't it great that He has given us the Bible as an instruction manual for a victorious life? He came to earth and walked among us, teaching us, guiding us, and finally dying for us. Life is such a pleasure when we live in the power and grace of God, knowing He has lifted us up out of the miry clay and planted us on a solid rock. Life lived in God's will is not a bum rap. It is a joy and privilege that should not be denied to anyone for any reason. We should thank God every day that He puts up with the error of our ways (even after He has given clear instructions) and helps us to keep on trying, even when we miss our intended goals.

All in all (and with her mother's help) my daughter turned out to be a pretty good driver. I just can't wait until my two granddaughters get to that age where they inquire, "Hey Mom, when can I get my permit so I can learn to drive?"

Dear Ole Dad

"Hear thou, my son, and be wise,
and guide thine heart in the way."
Proverbs 23:19

Growing up in Lick Skillet had its share of humorous moments. I'll never forget one incident that involved my dad. He was a good, hardworking individual who took care of his family and did his best to make sure all the bills were paid and his family was fed and sheltered.

He did have one character flaw: he was not the most patient man in the world. That one chink in his armor would prove to be a source of continual self-made difficulties throughout his life. But all in all he was quite a character, to say the least. His down-home humor, together with his willingness to help others, was always a source of joy when you were around him. You never knew what he was thinking or what he was going to say.

For example, when I graduated from seminary with my doctorate, the congregation of my church gave me a congratulatory reception in which many family, friends, and colleagues attended. One of those attendees was our director of missions and head of our local Baptist association. While there, the director politely said to my dad, "Mr. Fanning, I'm sure you are proud of that son of yours." To which my dad responded, "You mean him getting his doctor's degree? Well, between you and me, I hadn't got over him graduating from high school yet!"

On another occasion my dad was getting ready to leave for work. For some reason he was behind schedule and was frantically trying to shave, shower, and get dressed. All of a sudden we heard him use his strongest terminology ever, "DAD-BURN-IT!" Whenever he said "dad-burn-it" we knew it meant something serious. My mother ran in to see what had happened, only to find him rinsing his mouth in the bathroom lavatory. "What happened?" she asked. To which my father responded, "I grabbed that dad-burn tube of hair cream and brushed my teeth with it!" Back in those days there was a hair cream product that had for their slogan, "A little dab will do you!" He filled his mouth with more than a little dab that morning!

Someone once said, "Don't take life so seriously, you're not going to get out of it alive anyway." Doesn't this describe most of us? Far too often all of us are guilty of taking life w-a-a-a-y too seriously and we end up living in a perpetual state of stress and pressure. Most of us are in a hurry to get to our destination but cannot explain what the need to rush is. We live in a society where it appears that every little thing becomes a major crisis. It is during those times that we need to remember the words of Jesus as He explains, "Therefore I say unto you, take no thought for your life, what ye shall eat, or what ye shall put on. Is not the life more than meat, and the body than raiment? Which of you by taking thought can add one cubit unto his stature?" (Matthew 6:25–26).

Perhaps what we need more than anything right now is a reevaluation of our heart so we can determine who is actually in control of our lives. If self is on the throne of our life, we have great reason for concern. But if Christ is our Savior and Lord of our life, we have no reason to allow worry, doubt, and fear to defeat us. Truth is, all of us will be in eternity sooner than expected anyway. The apostle James said, "For what is your life? It is even a vapour, that appeareth for a little time, and then vanisheth way" (James 4:14).

If James is right (and he is) do you agree that life is just too short to allow the foolishness of scurrying around in a hectic society to drag you down? Remember: when it comes to worry, all it takes is a "little dab to do you in!"

Buckshot Bandit

"So is the man that deceiveth his neighbor, and saith,
Am not I in sport?"
Proverbs 26:19

Our community was, by-and-large, isolated from the bigger cities like Huntsville or Fayetteville during the days when I was growing up in Lick Skillet. Because of the distance, residents mainly purchased their goods locally; this accounted for a number of local mercantile stores spread throughout the county. Trips into the larger cities were rare, but when we did go it was a huge event. Most of the time the entire family would dress in their Sunday best, pile on the truck, and away we'd go. It was usually an all-day affair and one to which everybody looked forward.

Because of the vast farming industry, one of those precious commodities was the gasoline that kept all those tractors, trucks, combines, and other machinery operating. The farmers' weekly fuel supply was delivered and pumped into their personal tanks. Rarely was the tanker truck ever seen because most deliveries were made in the wee hours of the morning, usually around 2:00 a.m. This was so the farmer could begin his day without the stress of wondering if he had enough fuel to plow his fields. Each farm would receive a bill at the end of the month for the number of gallons received. The bill was either paid monthly or at the end of harvest season with one payment. Looking back, it is almost humorous when you consider the fact that gasoline was only twenty-one cents per gallon.

Unfortunately, these huge tanks were oftentimes sources of contention for the farmer because of fuel theft. In those early days, most Southerners either worked on the farm or had a job that was agriculturally related. Of course there were a few factories, construction companies, and food chains, but even these were dependent upon the success or failure of the farming industry.

The system worked great until there was a bad weather season. Sometimes there would be months before any work could be done because of heavy rains or drought conditions. These situations created a tremendous hardship on the field workers' families whose livelihood depended upon a weekly income. Not only that, but this also created a difficult dilemma for local merchants. Many of them had no choice but to extend a credit line to families who were supposed to pay either weekly, monthly, or make arrangements to settle accounts at the end of the harvest season. If there was no income many merchants were left with nothing more than a stack of unpaid credit slips. There were many situations where these farm employees would simply pack their belongings and move on during the night without saying a word to anyone.

It was during one of these crisis seasons when the entire South experienced a long, hot, and very dry summer. There was one farmer in our community by the name of Herman who experienced a confrontation that still causes me to smile when I think about it. In those days there was no such thing as air conditioning (unless you were a Methodist; they had an air-conditioned church). No household ever locked their doors and everyone slept with open windows. The crime rate wasn't as bad as it is today, so home break-ins were almost unheard of.

Anyway, as Herman was sitting in his easy chair listening to the evening news on the radio and hoping to get a positive report concerning the weather, his twelve-year-old nephew came in and said, "Uncle Herman, there's a guy outside standing next to your fuel tanks!" To which Herman asked, "Who is it and what is he doing?" The nephew responded, "Oh nothing, he is just leaned up against the tank with a bucket sitting next to him."

Immediately Herman understood what that meant—this guy was stealing tractor fuel! So he grabbed his old double-barreled 12-gauge shotgun and instructed his nephew to show him where he had seen the man. Carefully, Herman and his nephew maneuvered to a position where they could get a good look at the guy. And sure enough, there he stood, just as calm and confident as could be, leaning against that fuel tank and smoking a cigarette (apparently he was not very intelligent).

What happened next has become legendary in the Lick Skillet community. Herman yelled to the man, "Hey, what do you think you're doing?" The guy immediately took off running down a gravel road leading away from the barn. Herman yelled again, "Stop, or I'll shoot!" Of course the man didn't stop (would you?) but picked up his pace. He was out of sight in no time but you could hear his feet as they hit the loose gravel as he ran. Later, the nephew related to us that Herman raised that old shotgun and aimed in the direction of that crunching gravel and began counting... 1, 2, 3, 4... until he got to 10, then fired that old gun that was loaded with #8 bird shot. By this time the man had gotten far enough down the road that the buckshot only stung him with no serious injury, thus the reason for Herman's delay in pulling the trigger. The nephew said you could hear a faint "Yeo-w-w-w-w-w!" The guy yelled from a distance, "You so-and-so and so-and-so and so-and-so... (actually, there were lots more so-and-so's) ...you shot me."

There are those rare occasions when the good guy wins and the bad guy gets what he deserves. To be so earthly minded that we assume we can take what rightly belongs to others is a disaster in the making. Sin is a harsh taskmaster that continually demands unstinting obedience. It is a yoke that is cruel and severe and will ultimately lead to some serious consequences.

Determine to live in obedience to Christ, love your neighbors instead of taking advantage of them, and work hard at doing something *positive* instead of conniving and manipulating the circumstances to keep from working! Doing so just may save you the agony of a severe pain in your backside!

First-Class Outhouse

"It is better to dwell in the corner of the housetop, than with
a brawling woman in a wide house."
Proverbs 25:24

Living in the rural South, especially in the Skillet, was always a never-ending adventure. I've always found it humorous that many transferees from the North are astonished to find that we Southerners don't really comb our hair with a wagon wheel or brush our teeth with opossum fat. And contrary to popular belief, south of the Mason-Dixon we don't really get toothaches in our heels. Our women don't wear short burlap skirts and, yes, for the most part we do wear shoes. We don't believe that Jefferson Davis was ever president of the United States, and no, we are not saving our confederate money (at least most of us aren't) in hopes of the South rising again. We don't put roll bars in our cars or numbers on the doors, and we certainly don't yell "Yaaaahoooo" when we hit something. I admit that there may be a few other off-colored remarks uttered here and there but Yaaaahoooo? Never!

Back in the 50s and 60s, one thing that we Southerners did not possess (as did our northern counterparts) was the luxury of indoor plumbing. Before our northern friends faint dead away please know that we do have indoor plumbing today! Man, this new reformed South is something else. And just think, we have all you outsiders who have led us out of the wilderness and right straight to the promised land! I cannot believe the tremendous strides that have come our way in the past fifty years since all ya'll got here. Goodness, I don't think we ever would have learned how to drive in the snow if ya'll hadn't shown us the way! On behalf of Southern folks everywhere, from the depths of all our pea-pickin' hearts, thank ye, thank ye, thank ye! (I hope you don't mind, but I just had to take a side road to express my personal appreciation.)

Anyway, for us Southern folk, indoor plumbing was made possible with the invention of the mobile home. Back then they were called trailers. That was until Southern women got liberated and started wearing shoes. After that, referring to their home as a trailer became offensive and was considered politically incorrect. So manufacturers sawed the towing tongue off the front and took off the wheels at delivery and began referring to them as mobile homes. As time progressed and our culture got more dignified, we discovered we needed to change the name again. That is when the term *modular homes* became a watchword in Southern linguistics. And you just wait—even though I'm no prophet, I am predicting that if all this Southern prosperity continues, it will not take long for the name to change again. Can you say *versatile mansions?*

But up until about the 1960s most Southerners had an outhouse that was usually located about a quarter mile from the main dwelling (the reason for the distance should be obvious). The only problem with the distance was that it made it tough when your bodily functions kicked in, especially if there was snow on the ground or if you found yourself in a crisis in the middle of the night. It just isn't a pretty sight when you have to go in the dark and about halfway to the outhouse you accidentally step on a living creature or the dog sneaks up behind to bark or give you a cold nose. Most outhouses were a simple construction of sawmill run oak or pine. They generally had a roof, four sides, and a stool with one hole cut in the middle of a wooden plank that was built over a six-foot deep hand-dug hole in the ground. The construction of the stool was customized from family to family, depending on size and height of each individual. But the most important thing to remember in stool design was to make sure the "squat" height was equivalent to your family's need.

Another luxury these structures boasted (and that many are surprised to discover) is that they were actually heated and cooled. That's right! During the winter you would cover the cracks between the oak boards with burlap seed and feedbags to keep the wind out; during the summer you'd remove the burlap so you could feel the breeze.

Having an outhouse went much deeper than just a place where people took care of personal business. Many non-Southerners are surprised to learn that an outhouse was a good indication of a person's social status in the community. How these facilities were constructed was a testimony to a person's social or economic status within the community. Those who had a simple construction were considered lower class or common folk. If your outhouse consisted of any amount of concrete, shingles instead of a tin roof, or paint of any color, you were definitely labeled as middle or upper-middle class. If your outhouse had two or more holes and boasted 200 or more square feet, you were considered rich. If your outhouse had brick, wooden siding, or asbestos shingles—well—Donald Trump look out!

Usually, the kids at school whose parents owned the two-or-more-holer outhouses looked down on us one-holers. To this day I have emotional scars from the taunts and teasings from the two-holer crowd. That's something that takes *years* to get over without heavy counseling.

Anyway, now that you have a complete understanding of Southern outhouse trivia—a true story. It wasn't long after my wife and I were married that we attended a revival church meeting in rural Alabama. The little church was situated in a valley between two mountains, which required an hour-and-forty-minute drive on twisting rural roads. Actually these were nothing more than old logging trails around trees and huge rocks that had been paved.

When my wife and I finally got to the church we discovered we were first to arrive. And, as a result of our non-stop traveling excursion, my wife had to use the restroom.

Our arriving early presented two major problems. One, the only facility available was an old two-holer outhouse located about a quarter of a mile behind the church; and second, you couldn't get to it without crawling through a barbed-wire fence. Being the good, enterprising husband I am, I just pulled up the top strand of wire while placing my foot on the bottom strand and pushing down. This created a passageway through the fence and from there it was just a short hop to the outhouse.

She got through the fence just fine, but while she was in the outhouse the cows thought it was feeding time. About fifteen or twenty of them completely surrounded that outhouse with my wife inside. Meanwhile, I had gone back to the church to see if the doors were unlocked, and that is when I heard her yelling at the top of her lungs. Not realizing what had happened I ran back around the church as fast as I could. And there she was, the love of my life, peering out a crack in the doorway of that outhouse completely surrounded by cows that, I'm sure, were wondering what was wrong with this crazy female human.

Later, after she was rescued, I told her that at least she had a testimony to give during the service about her experience. I won't tell you how she responded to that, but I can assure you there was *no* testimony!

It wasn't long before all the people began showing up for church. That is when the best part of this story happened. As we walked in and began introducing ourselves to the congregation, one elderly lady walked over to my wife and whispered, "Honey, if you have to use the facilities, we just had a brand-new restroom built and it's on your right as you go down this hallway." That is when my wife gave me *the look* that clearly meant for me to never mention the outhouse incident again (I just hope she doesn't read this chapter!). Fact is, I learned some valuable lessons that day. First, that is what we get for going to a rich church that had a two-holer outhouse. Second, it got me to wondering why Southerners actually had two- and three-holers—for some reason that was never explained to me. I mean, I'm not acquainted with anyone that well, are you? And third, I learned that you don't have to use burlap bags now that caulking has finally made it to the South.

But, seriously, let this be a positive reminder about life. Life is much like our trip to that little church. Many times the road is long and winding with many boulders and obstacles in our way. However, persistence will eventually get you to your destination—and sometimes when you get there you find it isn't what you bargained for and certainly not even close to what you expected! I can assure you my sweet little wife never expected to be climbing through barbed wire to hike across a cow pasture to use a high-class two-holer outhouse! But you know what? Often, if we'll just be patient in our circumstances we will find that there's a brand-new shiny restroom just down the hallway!

How do you do that? How are we patient amid difficult and disappointing circumstances? Look at Jesus' response! Every time we see Jesus in a stressful situation we find Him going off to pray. Take a look at your Bible; I assure you that you'll find it there! Scripture often talks of Jesus going off to pray. Even on the most strenuous night of His life we find Him in great prayer in the Garden of Gethsemane.

Are you in the midst of an outhouse moment in life and feel you are surrounded with no way out? Take it to the Lord in prayer and trust Him to shoo the herd. He only works in your best interest!

Gun-shy Hunting Dog

"It is an honour for a man to cease from strife: but every
fool will be meddling."
Proverbs 20:3

One of my best friends while growing up in the Skillet
was Charley Edmondson. Charley was a wacky sort of
guy and just didn't see the world around him the way most
everybody else did. For Charley, he always saw humor in
every situation no matter how difficult, and he learned early
how to laugh at life. I suppose this is the reason why he was
so well liked by everyone in the community—he could
make you smile no matter what your circumstances.

To better help you understand how Charley's mind
worked, I remember one incident when he and I visited the
funeral home to show our respects to the family of a young
man who was tragically killed in an automobile accident.
Some of the church folk living in our community actually
thought this man's premature demise was the result of divine
judgment for his sins. See, he met his unfortunate end while
in the process of leaving town with another man's wife but
that is another story. Both he and his female companion were
instantly killed in a head-on collision with a drunk driver.

When Charley and I walked past the dead man's coffin we noticed that the body was dressed in overalls and a tee-shirt and he was wearing a ball cap with the words "Cat Diesel Power" on the front. I made a passing comment about how strange that was and Charley quietly responded, "Well, he is going to be lying there a long time and he might as well be comfortable!"

You know, it is just not good when you are looking down at an open coffin of the dearly departed while attempting to keep from bursting out laughing!!

Charley loved to quail hunt and was always buying, selling, and trading guns and bird dogs. On one occasion, Charley discovered an old rusty shotgun under the seat of a worn out pickup truck he had purchased. It didn't take him long to clean that old gun and immediately began proudly showing it off at the local mercantile store in downtown Skillet in hopes that someone might offer to buy it. Sitting beside the woodstove drinking an RC Cola was an old man who had been listening as Charley conveyed his story about the gun. Finally the man spoke up and said, "Tell you what, Sonny. I'll trade you a good hunting dog for that old shotgun." Charley responded, "Is he any good?" To which the old man responded, "Is he any good? Sonny, that dog is so good you have to place a patch over one of his eyes to keep him from trailing two coveys of quail at the same time!"

We all had a good laugh and Charley took the man up on his offer and traded the gun for the dog. The next day Charley called to ask me if I would like to go hunting with him so we could test his new dog's performance in the field. I told him I would and it wasn't long before Charley came driving up in his old 1978 Ford Ranchero with his new-found hunting dog sitting in the back.

Just in case you don't know what a Ford Ranchero is, it is a half car, half truck and sits low on the ground. It is important for you to understand this because this information will become very important in a few minutes. The vehicle cannot actually be classified as a truck, but neither is it a car. I guess the best way to describe it would be to simply say it is a Ford Galaxy with a truck bed on it.

We soon arrived at a cornfield and immediately Charley turned that dog loose so he could run around a little before proceeding to the hunt. We got our guns, ammunition, and hunting boots and headed across that cornfield with the dog following close behind. You also need to understand that a hunting dog following close behind is not a good sign. A good hunting dog is supposed to be out front sniffing and searching for quail.

I told Charley, "There is something wrong because he isn't acting like a prized hunting dog to me." To which Charley said, "You're right, but let's give him a chance and see if he gets better."

We walked for a good two miles and the entire time that dog followed sheepishly behind us every step of the way. By now Charley is getting really aggravated and had just about convinced himself that the old man back at the store had traded him a worthless dog for a rusty old shotgun (I thought the old man was the one who got the raw deal in the first place).

Just about the time we decided that dog was a dud, a covey of quail flew up immediately in front of us. Instinctively, both Charley and I raised our guns and simultaneously fired in the direction of that covey. Naturally we both missed, but all of a sudden we heard that dog yelp, cry, and howl. He tucked his tail between his hind legs and took off running like he was participating in a greyhound race. Charley was yelling for him to stop and for a moment I thought he was going to shoot that useless mutt. In a flash that dog was out of sight and neither of us could stop him.

Charley fussed and fumed all the way back to the spot where that Ranchero was parked. We didn't have a clue where that gun-shy dog had ended up, and frankly, neither of us really cared.

We finally got all our gear loaded in the truck (or car?) and were just about to leave when we both heard something like a low whine coming from underneath the vehicle. Charley asked, "Did you hear that?" and he immediately got out of the car and started searching for the mysterious sound. It didn't take long to discover the weird noise was the whines of that useless dog. Apparently, he was so frightened by the shotgun blast that he ran straight to the vehicle where he found refuge underneath that low-riding Ranchero. Charley got down on his hands and knees and was attempting to retrieve his dog by grabbing his collar. The problem was, the dog was lying about the center of the vehicle and because we were in a cornfield, plus the fact that the vehicle was so low to the ground, Charley couldn't reach him. He threw dirt clods at him, he tried to poke him with a long stick, he fired his gun in the air, he did everything he could think of but that dog wouldn't budge from underneath that truck.

Finally, in desperation, Charley had an idea. He slid under the steering wheel and started the engine. He thought the noise and heat might be a motivator for him to come out. We waited for a good long while but when that maneuver failed Charley put the truck in gear and began easing forward ever so gently, hoping to move the vehicle off the dog. I suppose the truck had gone approximately one hundred feet or so when Charley saw that the dog wasn't coming out. Confused, Charley opened the truck door and leaned over and looked underneath his truck so he could get a good look where his dog was. What he saw cracked us both up. That dog was hunched down like a combat soldier on the battlefield and was doing a belly crawl in conjunction with the movement of that truck.

We both fell on the ground laughing. Charley finally said, "Well, that dog may not hunt, but he sure is the smartest mutt I've ever owned." And with that the dog came crawling out from underneath that truck and straight to Charley like nothing had ever happened.

I've thought about that humorous incident many times over the years and I get a good laugh every time. But I also learned some things that are important. Over the course of my life I have found myself reacting to situations just like that dog. I've had tasks assigned, duties to perform, and work to do, but many times I end up letting others down by a poor performance. I've reconciled the problem in my own mind by convincing myself that it may have been an overestimation of my own abilities to do the job. Maybe it was fear that I wouldn't measure up or simple pride, arrogance, or my desire to live independent of what others say or want me to do.

Whatever the reason, all of us have a purpose in life. We must be willing to get into the heat of the battle and do our best to be what God designed us to be. Let's quit cowering under a false front and running for cover every time we hear the loud boom of responsibility. Also, let's quit holding others responsible when it is us who assigned a task that was beyond that person's ability to accomplish. At least they tried, and truly, that is all any of us can do.

We would do well to remember Deuteronomy 4:31, *"For the LORD your God is a compassionate God; He will not fail you nor destroy you."* Don't forget that God is on your team! He is your biggest cheerleader and not only does He desire your success in life, but is also paving the way for it! So, hold your head up high and don't cower under the Ranchero when things get tough or overwhelming! I assure you, if you'll make good use of that time you're spending underneath there on your knees, He will be there to usher you out!

The Trouble with Twins

"The man that wandereth out of the way of understanding
shall remain in the congregation of the dead."
Proverbs 21:16

A re you aware that scientists say that no two snowflakes
are exactly alike? Can you believe that?

I don't know about you, but that is hard for me to accept
as true. When I think about all the snowflakes in Iceland, the
South and North Poles, Alaska, and on all the mountaintops
of the world, and these guys are telling me that it is *impossible* to find two snowflakes exactly alike?

This immediately brings to mind several questions. First,
how do they really know that no two snowflakes are alike?
Are there *snowologists* with portable microscopes that go to
each snowdrift and examine each one? Second, what are the
criteria for such an examination? Are we talking rounded
points, variations in color and density, size, what?

And third, and maybe the most important, who really
cares anyway? The real question should be, "Don't these
people have better things to do than look at snowflakes day
in and day out?" Man, talk about getting a life!

Okay, where is this going and why even bring up the

subject? Well, are you aware that people are like snow-flakes? And, no, I don't mean they are *flakes!* I'm referring to the fact that no two people are exactly alike, even identical twins. No matter how much they have in common there will always be some noticeable differences in their physiological, psychological, and emotional makeup. Every individual has his/her own exclusive uniqueness.

When I was growing up in the Skillet two of my best friends were identical twins. If you weren't personally acquainted with them it was nearly impossible to tell them apart. They looked alike, dressed alike, and talked alike. They were also constant companions. If you saw one you automatically knew the other was close by.

When the twins attended grammar school at LSU (Lick Skillet University) they gave their teacher a basis for a mental breakdown. For example, she would ask a question in class and if the one called on didn't know the answer, the other would answer for him.

When the twins finally transferred to high school it was weeks before the administrative staff finally caught on to some of their shenanigans. Every other day one would go to school while the other would stay home. They got away with it for days by simply answering to each other's name as it was called in homeroom.

In my opinion, one of the most brilliant stunts the twins pulled was after the school administration decided that they could no longer be in the same class together. So the school counselor intentionally arranged their class schedules to keep them apart, thus making it easier for the teacher to identify them. But unknown to the faculty, one twin was strong in math and the other in science. So when the math teacher would announce a test in her class the twin that was strong in math would simply take the test for the other. They switched classes back and forth taking each other's tests for months until the guidance counselor finally figured out what they were doing.

It is easy to be somebody you are not. As a pastor I deal with people every day who, for the most part, do not like what they see in the mirror every morning. Our society is spending billions of dollars on clothing, make-up, exercise equipment, fad diets, etc, in our feeble attempts to transform ourselves into someone other than who God created us to be. I am not knocking good health practices and I am committed to exercise and proper nutrition. I believe the Bible makes it absolutely clear that we are to be responsible to take care of our bodies. The apostle Paul said, "Know ye not that ye are the temple of God, and that the Spirit of God dwelleth in you? If any man defile the temple of God, him shall God destroy; for the temple of God is holy, which temple ye are" (1 Corinthians 3:16–17 KJV).

A big untruth that is currently being propagated in our society is the "transformation on the outside transforms a person on the inside" philosophy.

Exercise gurus, diet promoters, and television talk show hosts are all pushing the idea that if we will just get our outward appearance in shape, do a complete make-over, lose 100 pounds, have plastic surgery, run twenty-five miles, cut out carbohydrates, purchase a thigh-buster, we will improve our self-image and be a better person inwardly.

The fact is, true freedom only occurs when we as individuals accept Jesus Christ as our Savior and recognize that God created us to be us. Does this mean that we are not to take care of our outward appearance? Absolutely not, but we do need to understand that a true outward transformation is only accomplished by a complete metamorphosis from the inside out, not the outside in. And this only occurs when the Holy Spirit indwells us the moment we accept Jesus as our personal Savior and are born again (John 3:3).

God views each of us as something special and He has a unique plan for your life that only you can fulfill. We are not an accident, a fluke, or a grain on the sandy beach of life. Instead, we are like the individual snowflake that is different from all the rest. We may resemble all the others on the outside, but closer observation reveals a unique masterpiece, one that plays its own distinctive role in creating the beauty of the snow-capped mountain landscape.

You may say, "I don't feel special or unique." But the truth is, most snowflakes will never be recognized individually, but together they make a stunning sight to behold. You may never be praised or publicly recognized by your fellow flakes (no pun intended) but God sees you as unique and He knows you by name. God sent His Son, Jesus Christ to give His life on the cross to obtain for you eternal salvation and help you realize your full potential here on earth. And what if you die? That is the good news. Because you have Jesus living on the inside, your life never really ends. One day you will simply move from an earthly existence over into the eternal and never miss a step. Isn't that good news?

So what about you? How do you see yourself? Are you living your full potential in Christ Jesus? Until you give your life in full surrender to Him and allow Him to transform you from the inside out you will never fully understand your full purpose in this life. Our new self-image is not found on a treadmill, in Botox injections, or by living on lettuce, oatmeal, and bottled water, but rather it is found in the person of Christ Jesus our Lord.

Rocking Reuben

"As he that taketh away a garment in cold weather, and as
vinegar upon nitre, so is he that singeth songs
to an heavy heart."
Proverbs 25:20

Being the pastor of a country church is a rewarding
experience but it can also have its more—well—stressful moments. Such was the case when our pastor received a
telephone call from a family in our community inquiring if
he would preside over a graveside funeral service. One of
their relatives had met an untimely demise as he was run
over by a city bus while crossing an Atlanta street.

Even though this family had deep roots in the community most of them had little to do with anything of a spiritual
nature. Not being associated with those *church people* was a
source of pride for the entire family and a convenient way of
dealing with a guilty conscience. According to them, attending church with *hypocrites* was just something that they had
no desire to do.

They did, though, make exceptions for church attendance
whenever special occasions such as weddings, Easter,
Christmas or an occasional *dinner on the grounds* or a fifth

Sunday *sangin'* arrived. Funerals were also excluded from their church attendance rule and I found it amusing that the father would always proudly proclaim, "I wouldn't be caught dead in a church with those self-righteous hypocrites!" That was a fine philosophy until one of his boys decided to run for mayor and needed votes. All of a sudden church attendance seemed really important!

Nonetheless on this occasion the family earnestly wanted their deceased cousin to be with his dearly departed kinsmen who were already buried there or would eventually have this as their final resting place.

The problem with this situation was that the departed man's wife had finalized her own funeral plans and had already cremated the body. Needless to say when the family discovered what the widow had done it created a great deal of frustration, fussing, and feuding, especially when they uncovered the fact that the deceased man and his current wife were in the process of getting a divorce just prior to his unfortunate demise.

So after a brief court hearing over who was the legal guardian of the deceased man's ashes a compromise was finally worked out. Eventually the judge ruled on their complaint and naturally the widow prevailed. But they reached a compromise on the deceased man's ashes. The widow did agree that she would turn the ashes over to the family for interment in whatever manner they felt fitting. In other words, she got the money and they got her honey, which was a possession that she was more than happy to surrender.

Looking back I suppose the family felt some justification because rumor was that the ex was planning on renting an airplane and spreading his ashes either across the Appalachian Mountains (of which the deceased had never seen) or over the Atlantic Ocean (over which he had never been). Somebody said that she got the idea while watching a movie and she was so moved by that compassionate scene that she vowed when Ruben died she would do the same. Anyway the day finally arrived for the long-awaited funeral and our pastor was instructed to be at the cemetery around 11:00 a.m. to say a few comforting words over Ruben's ashes. I never asked him, but I suppose that pastor must have looked through his Bible for hours attempting to find a fitting Scripture that fit this occasion. What do you say about a guy who left his family, ran off to Atlanta, married a woman of questionable character, and got run over by a city bus? About the only appropriate Scripture one could use would be something similar to Proverbs 26:8, "Like one who binds a stone in a sling is he who gives honor to a fool."

In any case the pastor arrived at the cemetery in plenty of time to offer his condolences to the grieving family. He was told that the ashes were being transported from Atlanta by car driven by one of the cousins and should arrive any moment. As they waited the family visited around the various family gravestones and reminisced about days past. Some of the children found a nearby stream and were busy playing in the water while their mothers were constantly badgering them about not getting their new clothes wet or dirty.

Minutes ran to hours and still no ashes. Some non-family members became weary of the wait and began leaving the cemetery. Finally one of the uncles walked over to our pastor and said, "Preacher, we don't know what has happened but we understand if you have to leave." The pastor responded with graciousness but politely declined and reassured the family that he would wait for the ashes with them.

It was about this time that a police cruiser came driving up the long winding road to the gravesite. When the officer got out of his automobile he walked over to one family member and whispered something softly to him. The family member looked immediately in the direction of the pastor and said, "Preacher, I need for you to please come with me. There has been an accident!" The pastor and some family members immediately got in the cruiser with the police officer and headed back down the cemetery road.

Weeks later the pastor privately shared with my dad what had happened. The cousin that was transporting the ashes was almost to the cemetery when they had to stop at a four-way intersection. While stopped, a huge farm truck loaded with soybeans accidentally hit the rear of their car thus dislodging the container of old Ruben's ashes. Unfortunately for the family, the urn's lid came off with *strewn Ruben* all over the trunk of that new car as a result. When the pastor arrived at the accident scene he discovered the cousin in the process of sucking up poor old cousin Ruben with a little Dirt Devil vacuum cleaner, attempting feverishly to get as much of him back in that urn as possible.

Now let us pause here for a moment while I ask you a personal question. Have you ever experienced one of those occasions when you started laughing and even if your life depended on it you couldn't stop? That is exactly what happened to our pastor. He became so hysterical at the sight of that cousin sucking up Ruben's ashes that it became necessary for him to lean against the automobile for physical support. This in turn infuriated the family who immediately demanded that the pastor leave the premises.

It didn't take long for word to get back to the community what had happened and of course the entire story had taken on a brand-new twist by the time it had made its rounds. It didn't matter though. The next Sunday the deacons met to decide what needed to be done about their laughing pastor. Apparently the offended family had complained to some of the deacons and because of kinships, friendships, etc., everyone knew there was no way the pastor could be an effective man of God in their community again. They searched in vain through the Scriptures attempting to come up with some biblical reason to dismiss him. I don't think that laughing at a funeral was dealt with in the Ten Commandments and Jesus never made reference to it in the New Testament either. One of them quoted Ecclesiastes 2:2, "I said of laughter—madness: and of mirth, what does it accomplish?" But the pastor countered with Proverbs 14:13, "Even in laughter the heart may sorrow, and the end of mirth may be grief."

When it was all said and done it didn't make much difference because the pastor was let go from his position and wasn't allowed to minister to his congregation from that point on.

While sharing this event with my dad the pastor said that now whenever he either attends or preaches a funeral he is reminded that in a cemetery in North Alabama there are ashes of a man named Ruben buried in a Dirt Devil vacuum cleaner bag. And without fail he would smile and believe that, "Be not deceived; God is not mocked: for whatsoever a man soweth, that shall he also reap" (Galatians 6:7).

Living the High Life

"Enter not into the path of the wicked, and go not in the
way of evil men."
Proverbs 4:14

Life in the Skillet wasn't always a pleasant valley
Sunday. Like everyone, there were those times when
you woke up in the morning lying between the wall and the
bed and you wondered if you needed make the effort to get
up at all. Somehow, you just knew that today wasn't going
to be your day!

Such was the case one New Year's Eve when one of the
locals, a guy named Bob, decided to celebrate in a big way.
Old Bob spent the entire night saturating his brain with a
mixture of 100-proof whiskey and chasing it with 12-ounce
cans of beer. Now, I'm not a drinker and never have been,
but I've been around long enough to know that this had to be
a bad combination—especially when you mix alcohol with
driving a 1964 Pontiac GTO with a 389 cubic inch V8 and
four-speed transmission!

Bob's drinking binges weren't anything new for it was
common knowledge among the locals that he was prone to
indulge occasionally. Unfortunately for Bob, he just didn't

know when to stop once he started. Rumor in the community was that his drinking was the result of some horrible experiences while serving in the Army during the Vietnam War. I don't recall anyone asking him if that was true and I'm fairly certain he wouldn't have answered it anyway. Whatever the reason, once Bob began drinking he just didn't have the ability to know when he'd had enough. Once he started, you weren't really sure if he was going to be your friend or your enemy.

One Saturday I saw Bob at a local hardware store and could immediately discern that he wasn't feeling well. "Hey Bob, you don't look so good. What's wrong?" I asked. He responded, "Man, I've already had a rough weekend and it's only Saturday morning. Last night I went across the state line to a club and they fixed me a drink called a Harvey Wallbanger. I'm not sure what they put in it, but I know now why they call it that!"

Anyway, on this New Year's Eve the local PTA was sponsoring a fireworks display at LSU (Lick Skillet University). Everybody in the Skillet came out to see the show, including Bob. The only difference between them and him was that by the time he got there he was already higher than those rockets they were launching and he was yelling and hollering at everybody. One minute he would be crying and blubbering about his long-lost mother and the next moment he wanted to fight some guy that he said looked at him weird.

But before the fireworks show ended, Bob was feeling really good and was offering to buy the entire community a drink. At one point he somehow made his way to the stage and got hold of a microphone. He began crying again and wanted everyone present to know how much he loved them and that he considered all of us as his best friends.

Well, the fireworks display ended and everyone had a good time. Bob staggered to his car and climbed behind the wheel of that powerful Pontiac GTO. He revved the engine, turned a few donuts in the school parking lot and peeled out of there like one of those rockets we had just seen launched. Apparently, because he was under the influence, the power of that Pontiac proved to be more than Bob would handle and he lost control. One individual, who witnessed the wreck, said the car flipped end over end at least seven times before coming to a stop resting on its top. That car was traveling so fast that it ended up approximately 100 yards in the middle of a cotton field. Everybody running toward the scene wouldn't have given a wooden nickel for Bob's life at that moment.

The first group to arrive at the car was fully expecting to pull Bob's lifeless body from that tangled mess of metal. What they witnessed when they got there has been a source of conversation within the community for years. For they found Bob standing on the top (or bottom since that is what was turned upward) auctioning off to the highest bidder what remained of his GTO. And he also just wanted everyone to know how much he appreciated this tremendous turnout for his auction.

Looking back on that event causes me to reevaluate my own life. I believe if I could live my life over again that there would be several things that I would do differently and some things I would not do at all. I certainly do not advocate drinking alcohol or abusing drugs of any sort. To do so usually results in a premature death or at least causes us to make fools out of ourselves. But I do think I'd try to make fewer mistakes the next time around. I believe I would relax more and try to be sillier than I have on this go around. I would take more trips and try to talk my wife out of packing thermometers, Metamucil, aspirin, Pepto-Bismol, a hot water bottle, raincoat, bathmat and a parachute. I'd climb more mountains, fish more, and watch more sunsets. Instead of walking for my health, I would try walking for the scenery. I would listen to my elders' advice and play with children more. I would eat lots more ice cream and a lot less health food. I'd be more concerned about my fellowman and less concerned about my waistline. I would have fewer imaginary troubles. I would put less emphasis on the accumulation of things and stuff and more on family and sharing. If I had it to do over again, I would travel more, do things like riding a merry-go-round, picking daisies, and spending more time in a clover field.

I truly believe life is what you make it. Isn't it sad that there are people who feel they must endure life instead of enjoying it? Many can't seem to survive unless they get that false sense of security they can only find in a bottle or a pill.

Remember, Jesus said, *"I am come that they might have life, and that they might have it more abundantly"* (John 10:10 KJV). Why don't you take Him at His word and start enjoying life from a spiritual perspective without the aid of outside crutches like alcohol and unnecessary drug use? I believe you will find that you can love yourself as well as others a lot better.

Double-Dog Dare

"The lips of the righteous feed many:
but fools die for want of wisdom."
Proverbs 10:21

I've been miserable for a couple of weeks now and, to be honest, it is my own fault. Well, maybe it is not ALL my fault! Actually, I've decided that I am what sociologists might call horticulturally challenged (in other words I don't know beans when it comes to plants). Please allow me to explain. It all started with this huge oak tree that is located in my backyard. For years it has had these weird vines growing around it to the point they have almost consumed the entire tree. So this past weekend I decided that I needed to do something about it. I got up early on Saturday morning, put on my old work clothes, ate breakfast, then grabbed my weed-eater and walked to the base of that giant oak. It didn't take me but a few yanks on the cord and almost immediately the RPMs on that little weed-whacker were at approximately 10,000. Like a wild man with a vengeance I lit into that offensive growth like there was no tomorrow. It strewed vines, branches, and green leaves all over everything that was within a quarter mile (slight exaggeration). Those vines were green, shiny, and also filled with a white liquid that completely covered me as well as my little weed-whacker.

Okay, I'll admit it. I really did know that those vines were poison ivy, but in all my years on this earth I have never had an allergic reaction to that stuff. That is, until now.

My recent experience with those poison ivy vines rekindled a distant memory of when I was in the seventh grade at LSU (Lick Skillet University). One day a group of us boys were gathered around a similar-looking oak tree behind the school that was also covered with those same vines. It wasn't long before somebody said, "I double-dog dare any one of you to grab hold of that poison ivy and rub it on your face." We never verbalized it, but we thought it was a stupid idea. Finally, after we didn't respond, this same bozo retorted, "That's what I thought, all of you are chicken!" About that time another kid said, "Hey, if you are so brave, let's see you do it!" To which bozo boy said, "I'll do it if you will." Without further ado, he walked over and grabbed a handful of poison ivy leaves and began to rub them all over his face, hands, legs, and just about everything else he had exposed. Not to be outdone, all of us repeated this idiotic stunt and when we were done, another challenge was issued, "Anybody who washes it off is a scum-bagging, dirty, yellow-dog coward!" That sealed it—not a single one of us wanted to be labeled as a scum-bagging, dirty, yellow-dog coward; so we didn't dare wash it off.

Everything seemed fine for the remainder of that day with the exception of us suspiciously watching each other to make sure we didn't secretly wash. But from all appearances it looked as though we had all made it without any problems, thus proving we weren't scum-bagging, dirty, yellow-dog cowards.

That is, all was fine until my parents received a telephone call later that evening from the mother of one of my friends. Apparently, one of my fellow yo-yos was so swollen that he had to be rushed to the emergency room. I guess he was in such agony that he finally confessed what had happened at school and the hospital personnel gave her instruction to call all the parents to see if we were okay. I listened as my mother said, "You have got to be kidding! Why, that is the dumbest thing I have ever heard. What possessed those boys to do such a dim-witted thing?"

If memory serves me correctly I think that three out of five of us boys ended up with severe allergic reactions to the poison ivy. For me, I never so much as got a red spot! The only thing that was red on me was my backside when my dad finished putting me in time out!

That incident occurred over forty years ago and all of a sudden here I am today—an itching, scratching, miserable parody of a human being. And I'm not sure, but I think even the weed-whacker has a rash! Isn't it interesting that all these years have passed and I'm just now at the place where poison ivy stirs an allergic reaction in my body?

Did you know that the Bible teaches this same principle when it comes to the subtleness of sin? What begins as a perceived insignificant nothing can quickly escalate into a huge, gigantic something. An alcoholic's life always begins with a simple taste, many times on a dare from friends. Many drug addicts began their habit with a sampling of marijuana just to show they can fit in with the popular crowd. Many have either prematurely died, or are dying, from cancer and heart disease because they thought it was cool to smoke as a teenager. Every sinful habit you can name begins with a subtle, insignificant attitude that says, "Just a little surely won't hurt!"

The apostle Paul stated it plainly when he said, "Professing themselves to be wise, they became fools" (Romans 1:22).

But there is one thing we can always count on when it comes to doing dumb things. Our dim-witted decisions may not have caused us to become alcoholics or drug abusers. And we may not be dying from a dreaded disease because of a momentary lapse in judgment. And yes, there just may be that outside chance that we dodged a bullet and thankfully got by with something others did not. But there is one thing they cannot say about us—at least we are not a scumbagging, dirty, yellow-dog coward! Right?

Not-So-Holy Baptism

"Happy is the man that findeth wisdom, and the man that
getteth understanding."
Proverbs 3:13

Whether you are an eternal optimist, or whether you
believe in Murphy's Law (if it can go wrong, it will),
you have to agree that more often than not things do go
wrong! Such was the case with one of my first baptisms
early in my ministry.

Being the pastor of a small country church I realized the
seriousness of the moment and truly desired for this baptism
to be done correctly. The little church was a beautiful, small
brick building nestled in a lovely valley between two mountains and was picture-postcard pretty, especially during the
peak of autumn. However, there was one very unique
attribute to this otherwise perfect parish: the baptistery was
situated in the floor *beneath* the choir! I had never seen a
design like it and always admired the congregation's
attempts to utilize their useable floor space. Personally
though, I think I would have been a little uncomfortable
singing in the choir knowing that the only thing separating
me from a good dunking in 2,000 gallons of water was a

one-inch pine board under my feet. It did not seem to bother them, and if they were comfortable with it, who was I to interfere? Man, talk about faith! The unique baptistery design created somewhat of a problem whenever there was a baptism. All the men of the congregation would assemble at the front and begin removing the choir chairs. They would then carefully lift the hinged floor that covered the baptistery, thus exposing the baptismal waters. Then the pastor and baptismal candidate would walk down into the pool while the remainder of the congregation crowded around as best they could to observe.

On one occasion I was baptizing a lady who, for some reason, would not submerge under the water. I'm not exaggerating! When I would bend her backwards to dunk her under, her feet and head would be level with the water line. It was like attempting to baptize a two-by-four or a wooden canoe. She simply would not go under the water! That is when I began to panic and started trying to figure out what I was going to do. I immediately thought back to my seminary training, trying to recall one class that might have dealt with this situation! Surely in the midst of all that theology, eschatology, psychology, and every other "ology" there had to be something. Well, there wasn't and I knew I was going to have to figure this one out on my own.

I had already observed that when I put her head under the water, her feet would come up and stick out above the water line. And when her feet would go down, her head would come up! I could literally rock her back and forth and make her bobble up and down like a cork. Finally, being a young, enterprising pastor (not to mention temporarily insane), I became so completely absorbed with getting this lady under the water that I overlooked my ministerial ethics. I placed one hand behind her neck and the other on her chest and gave that lady a mighty downward shove. And that's when it happened! When she went under I couldn't believe the chain reaction that occurred. The biggest, most destructive air bubble in the history of mankind rushed to the surface sending that dear lady's skirt up over her head and nearly drowning me and all those poor souls who were intently and prayerfully observing. It also made a weird *whooooshing* sound, the cause of which, to this day I'm not certain. Later, some testified that it sounded to them like the sound of a freight train (that's how people in the South describe any disaster). But I am convinced of one thing: it had to be the same sound that surely accompanied the sinking of the Titanic back in 1912. To compound the problem even more, when the water rushed in to fill that air pocket, that woman slipped out of my wet hands and immediately sank completely to the bottom of the baptistery. It truly was a sight to behold. One minute she seemed to have been supernaturally suspended above water; the next she was sinking like a rock! In my mind it seemed like all this lasted for an eternity.

Finally, I got hold of her and with much straining and grunting on my part, I got her back to the surface and on her feet. And the most amazing thing was that the lady didn't realize that anything was wrong! She had her eyes closed and her hands folded in her spiritual posture and remained that way all the way to the bottom and back to the top again. I don't think she ever knew how close she came to having the pastor and deacons organize a search and rescue team right then and there!

I suppose it was the devil, but as I pondered the event later, I couldn't help but smile as I considered if things had gone differently. How would I have explained the emergency to a 911 operator? What if she had drowned? Can you imagine a Baptist congregation giving their version of events to a grand jury? They would have had to call a meeting and organize a drowning committee to look into the situation. They also would have to discuss the problem over a fellowship meal. And probably, if they are like most Baptist churches, the pastor would have to be let go because that was not the way we've always done it!

Anyway, when I finally got the lady back on her feet, her skirt had found its way back to its proper place and I was grinning like a schoolboy for accomplishing the impossible. It was at this moment, as I stood there out of breath, soaked to the skin and wondering if I'd mistaken God's calling on my life, that I suddenly remembered all those people in the congregation who were still standing right above me observing all this. I realized that I had become so involved with saving this lady's life that I had totally forgotten about them. When I looked up, all I saw and heard were sniggering and lame attempts to restrain their laughter. Everybody was holding their sides and trying to keep from bursting out in laughter while attempting to sing the old hymns of the faith while maintaining *their* spiritual posture at the same time.

Over the years I've given that strange baptismal service a lot of thought and have come to some interesting conclusions. First, I'm convinced that to survive this life one must have a healthy sense of humor. We live in a world that is literally falling apart with violence, tragedy, natural, and not-so-natural disasters. To cope, without losing our sanity, we must develop an emotional outlet to deal with the problems around us. We need to understand that life has its light moments and we ought to take full advantage of these rare times and laugh a little. Second, I'm convinced that we all spend too much time dwelling on the bad while overlooking the good. I'm not suggesting that we laugh in the face of danger or tragedy, I'm saying we need to try to find good in every bad situation.

Finally, I don't know what it's going to be like when I die and stand before the Lord, but it wouldn't surprise me one bit if Jesus hits the rewind button on my life and reruns that baptismal incident a few times.

So come on and lighten up! Only a fool deceives himself into thinking he is not going to have to take a few knocks and bumps in life. Remember, it's not the difficult storms on the outside that we need to dwell on, but rather there is a Savior on the inside who will aid us to discover the bright side of our difficult circumstances. Learn the secret of not taking life so seriously that you miss the joy of living.

Need for Speed

"Can one go upon hot coals, and his feet not be burned?"
Proverbs 6:28

My mother's sister married a guy who was a life-long resident of Lick Skillet. His father operated a convenience store approximately one mile from the main drag in downtown Skillet. I've got to admit that life changed for our family after that marriage took place. His love for speed, coupled with a deep desire to race motorcycles and automobiles, convinced my grandfather that his newly acquired son-in-law had a secret, subconscious desire to commit suicide. I just always believed he was nuts and let it go at that.

This guy always seemed to find humor in the most unlikely places. He also seemed to have a talent for convincing me to participate in some questionable and hair-brained projects he'd concocted. Like the day he asked me to steer an old 1959 Studabaker Hawk automobile that he'd traded for.

The car had no engine or transmission and had to be towed by another vehicle. Unfortunately, the means by which he chose to accomplish this task was a 20-foot log chain and a 1956 Chevy pickup truck that had been modified with a 400 hp engine. To say that this was overkill is an understatement to say the least. After convincing me that I had nothing to worry about, we commenced towing that old Studabaker from Lick Skillet to his brother's service station in Huntsville where he had plans of installing a huge 472 cubic-inch Cadillac engine in that old Studabaker Hawk. Things went fairly well for the first couple of miles, but when we got to the intersection of Charity Lane and Highway 231 that modified pickup with that 400 hp engine (as well as a lack of good common sense) took over. It wasn't long before we were clipping along at a good 80 miles per hour. I was yelling, stepping on the brake, and wanting to cry but was either too proud or too stupid to do so. When my uncle would come upon a slower automobile and necessitated a lane change he would simply hang his arm out the window and point left. If we needed to cross back into the right lane he would hold up his arm and point over the cab of the truck, gesturing for me to follow him back over.

For some unknown reason as we were easily moving from 80 mph to 95 mph, I couldn't help but remember a story that I had heard years earlier. It was the story of a kid on a bicycle who had wandered far from home and realized he was too tired to pedal the return trip. Wondering what to do, he finally had a brilliant idea. He walked over to a parked car and asked a man if he wouldn't mind if he tied his bicycle to the back bumper of the Cadillac with a rope. The man thought for a moment and finally agreed, but gave him one warning. "If I get too fast, just blow the horn located on your handlebars and I'll slow down." Off they went with things going as planned. It wasn't long before the man in the car got into a race with another vehicle and completely forgot about the kid on the bicycle that was tied to his rear bumper. Soon they passed a road sign with a policeman hidden behind it with a radar gun. The policeman was so shocked by what he saw that he got on his police radio and said, "Sarge, you're not going to believe this, but there's two cars racing and headed your way." The police sergeant responded, "What's so unusual about that?" The policemen responded, "Because if you think they're going fast, wait until you see that kid on the bicycle behind them blowing his horn, wanting to pass!"

As I've thought about that situation over the years, I am reminded that life is really a process of growing and maturing, more than a list of answers or quick advice. I feel that we learn more from experiences, both good and bad, than we will ever learn from verbal instruction.

Do you remember what Jesus said to His disciples just before He was crucified? "I have yet many things to say unto you, but ye cannot bear them now. Howbeit when he, the Spirit of truth, is come, he will guide you into all truth" (John 16:12–13).

A final word: be short on advice and long on encouragement. Be slow to give answers, but quick to help others discover them. Make every situation a learning experience. And more importantly—beware of allowing crazy relatives to convince you to do something you know you shouldn't!

Motorcycle Miracle

"Ponder the path of thy feet, and let all thy ways
be established."
Proverbs 4:26

One of the most amazing spectacles I ever witnessed occurred one Thanksgiving Day in 1974. All my aunts, uncles, cousins, grandparents, neighbors, homeless, stray dogs, and just about everybody on earth gathered at my aunt and uncle's house for a day of fun, food, and family activities. It was certainly a day to remember; however, I didn't realize at the time just how unforgettable it would turn out be—especially for my brother-in-law.

It all began when one of my uncles showed up at the event with a truckload of off-road motorcycles. We immediately began choosing which one each of us would ride but soon discovered that we were one short. Another one of my uncles (whose house where we had gathered) finally said, "I have one in the garage if somebody wants to ride it." We walked to his garage and discovered it was an old Honda street bike that had the mufflers and both front and rear fenders sawed off. It was a pitiful looking old thing and was definitely not built for trail riding. But my brother-in-law was desperate and in this situation the old Honda would have to do.

All day my bother-in-law lagged behind those sleek trail bikes, which, in turn, forced all of us to have to stop from time to time to allow him to catch up. You could hear him coming a mile away with those sawed-off mufflers so there was never any danger of him getting lost. All day he griped, fumed, and complained about having to ride that old bike, but was determined not to let the rest of us get too far ahead. He attempted everything from bribery to outright physical violence, trying to make a bike trade with one of us that day. Unable to succeed in a trade he finally realized that he was stuck with that Honda. I'm not sure, but I think it was his determination to keep up with the rest of us that finally got him into trouble.

We had been riding across the fields and through forest for about two hours when we came upon a steep terrace on the rough terrain. As each of us hit that terrace, the bike would literally fly for some distance before settling gently back to earth again. That is, until we heard my brother-in-law coming fast and hard on that old Honda.

We were all standing on the opposite side of the terrace waiting to see how he would fare in flight. And sure enough, just as that old Honda got airborne, my brother-in-law came off the seat and immediately went into an unintentional handstand on the handlebars! Both of his feet were in the air and his entire body was completely parallel in an upside down position as he desperately hung on. My uncle, who owned the bike, started yelling, "He's going to make it! He's going to make it" thinking he might actually return to a seated position. Unfortunately for my brother-in-law, he came all the way over those handlebars, resulting in his devouring at least fifty pounds of plowed dirt (personal exaggeration). As he and his motorcycle shot past us hopping and bopping, rockin' and rolling at what seemed to be all night long, my uncle sadly said, "Oh well, I guess he didn't make it!" When we got to him that boy was skinned from head to toe, clothes torn, teeth rattled. I've seen road kill that looked better.

So what has all this got to do with anything? I can think of several things. First, I'm just thankful that my brother-in-law recovered and wasn't hurt too badly. Second, I want to thank him for teaching me that life has its rough spots. Third, life sometimes means making do with what you have. Fourth, try to talk your sister out of marrying a guy who doesn't know his ups from his downs! And fifth, I'm just finally glad that I'm writing about something that didn't happen to me!

Not-So-Bright Move

"As vinegar to the teeth, and as smoke to the eyes,
so is the sluggard to them that send him."
Proverbs 10:26

For most folks, growing up in the rural South automatically gave you an association with cotton in one way or the other. You either picked cotton, lived next to a cotton field, or at least you wore cotton clothing. Nowadays, most people's association with the cotton industry is just simply to be sprayed with deadly chemicals from the crop duster planes that fly over their house.

Before the modern era, field workers labored from dawn to dusk dragging huge cotton sacks and picking cotton by hand. The work was hard and tedious and most everyone did their fair share by working in the fields. Back then, even schools would close during harvest time so the kids could help. Everything revolved around the cotton industry. We had cotton parades, crowned cotton queens, and had bumper stickers that said, *"I LOVE COTTON!"*

Picking cotton by hand meant bleeding hands, bruised and scraped knees, aching backs, and enduring 100-degree days dragging a cotton sack that, at full capacity, could weigh as much as 200 pounds. Those were definitely old times that were not forgotten!

There's no doubt about it, cotton was revered as king and the chief source of revenue in the South for decades; you either loved it or left it!

Today, cotton is still a major commodity in the South but it is not her bread and butter like it used to be. Nonetheless, the sight of a 1,000-acre cotton field stretching as far as the eye can see is indeed a beautiful sight to behold. Thankfully, the days of field hands dragging a cotton sack are over and have been replaced by giant mechanized cotton pickers. These intimidating looking machines inch slowly across pure white fields equipped with hundreds of rotating steel fingers gathering as much cotton in one day that twenty-five field hands used to cover in a week.

The year after I graduated from high school I worked for a short time on a large cotton farm. One of my duties was to operate a cotton picker. One day I witnessed a spectacle that, to this day, breaks me up when I think about it. As I explained earlier, a cotton picker has hundreds of rotating steel fingers that pull the cotton from the cotton boll. But for the cotton to separate cleanly from the boll there are hundreds of gallons of water mixed with a washing detergent that pours over those rotating steel fingers to keep them moist. Several times a day the water tank that is mounted on the cotton picker has to be refilled and detergent added to keep the picker operating smoothly. In our case, we had an old one-ton, 1952 Chevy truck (it was a low-budget operation) that had a huge 2,000-gallon water tank mounted on the bed. Needless to say, when that water tank was full it was all that old Chevy truck could handle. The stopping distance was—well—nearly impossible and had to be done carefully and with much forethought.

One day the farmer's son and I were operating pickers in the same field. Taking care of the water truck was a man who wasn't the greatest driver in the world. Matter of fact, he had his license suspended because of too many reckless driving incidences.

Anyway, the water level in the truck tank was nearly empty and in need of replenishing. This task usually took at least two hours which meant that either the farmer's son or I would need to park one of the cotton pickers and go refill the water tank. On this day we were behind schedule and needed to get those two cotton fields in which we were currently working harvested before dusk. Finally, as we were arguing over who would go, this guy spoke up and said, "I'll do it!" We both looked at each other and he finally, with lots of reluctance, we agreed to let this guy drive the tanker truck down to the river to get the much-needed water. The last thing we said to the guy was, "Look, just be careful and get back as soon as you can! You know we have got to get these fields done before dark."

Someone once said time is a precious thing! I'm not exactly sure that was the case with us that day. About an hour after we allowed that guy to go fill the water tank, my picker depleted its water supply and I had to stop until it could be replenished. It wasn't long before the same happened on the other cotton picker as well. We both moved our machines to the end of those long cotton rows and sat there in the swelter-ing sun waiting for that water truck to return. We waited, we waited, and we waited some more. Finally, after about three hours, the farmer's son said, "You know, I'll bet that guy has gotten that truck stuck in the mud and can't get out! Let's get in the pickup and go check on him."

We hadn't traveled but a quarter of a mile when we spied him walking toward us, completely soaked from head to toe. All we could say at that point was, "Oh no!" When we got to him all the man said was, "Did you know the brakes on that truck don't work?" At that point I deducted, "This is going to be much worse than we thought!"

When we got to the river we couldn't see that tanker truck anywhere. About this time the farmer's son asked, "Well, where is the truck?" The man simply pointed in the direction of the river. Sure enough, what first appeared to be a big rock in the middle of the river turned out to be about six-inches of the top section of the cab on that 1952 submerged Chevy truck. And the huge 2,000-gallon water tank had already floated downstream and was probably in China by that time.

We were all three standing by the water's edge attempting to figure out what to do next when the farmer, returning from purchasing supplies, happened to be traveling down that very road.

Before we proceed with this story, it is important that you realize the old farmer suffered from severe asthma and could hardly breathe, much less yell. He looked at us, saw that guy who was still soaked from head to toe, and then spied that nearly submerged water truck. Believe me, you didn't have to tell him what had happened. Right then and there he mentally put it all together and came out of his truck like the space shuttle off the launching pad. He got to yelling so loud and became so upset that his asthma kicked in and he lost every breath of air he had and was forced to sit down for a moment to collect himself. He heaved, wheezed, sniffed, and snorted, and I thought he was going to that great cotton field in the sky any second. He would sit long enough to get some air and collect himself then would fly into another wheezing, snorting rage. Finally, his son forced him into the cab of his truck and headed for home. The entire time the farmer was hanging out the passenger window of that pickup with his son clutching tightly to the rear of dad's pants attempting to keep him from jumping out. You could hear him yelling to the top of his lungs long after they got out of sight.

They were not gone for very long before the farmer's son returned with a big tractor so we could finally get that water truck pulled from the river. And since the hired hand was still soaked, guess who got to go underwater and secure that tow chain to the submerged front bumper on that truck? Once the chain was connected and the other end hooked to the tractor we easily pulled the truck from the river. The weird thing was that we never recovered the 2,000-gallon water tank. We searched for weeks but apparently it just disappeared into oblivion. Come to think of it, I never again saw nor heard from the guy that caused all the commotion to begin with either. Maybe the two disappearances are connected, who knows?

What is the moral of this story? Well, let's see. How about (1) Never assume people can do the job simply because they volunteer. (2) If you are going to submerge your truck make sure it is in fresh water. (3) Be careful not to get in too deep or you'll be overwhelmed. (4) When you go get supplies take another route home. (5) Talking on a cellular phone while driving is a lot easier than holding your daddy in the truck by the seat of his pants.

Butter Bean Back-Talkin'

"Whoso loveth instruction loveth knowledge: but he that
hateth reproof is brutish."
Proverbs 12:1

In 1960, when I was eight, I made the foolish mistake of
back talking my mother. Simply sitting here today writing about it gives me cold chills and a sick feeling in the pit
of my stomach. Experiences like that have a tendency to
stick in your mind and cause all sorts of strange phenomena
to dance around in your head once you're an adult. It took
years of therapy before counselors finally convinced me that
this experience was only the result of a simple case of
temporary insanity on my part.

Let me explain. Back in the 60s and 70s things were a
lot different than they are today. Kids didn't have the freedom to sass or trash mouth their parents or even raise their
voices in anger or defiance. The very thought of saying *no*
to your father or mother or your refusal to perform a task
when assigned never entered a kid's thought patterns. Back
then, you couldn't be disrespectful to your parents and live
to tell about it. If you did happen to slip up or you just plain
forgot, you were either shot at sunrise or you were banished

103

from your home. Some sociologists theorize that this is where the hippie movement of the 1960s began. These were all kids who had to leave home with no place to hide because they had talked back to their parents. For some unknown and mysterious reason, they all simultaneously ended up at Woodstock, New York to rebel against this rotten establishment.

Child rearing in the 60s and 70s had a completely different meaning than it does today. For example, "time out" back then was defined as "a state of prolonged unconsciousness brought on by extreme physical and mental stresses." In other words, "time out" was the amount of time you were rendered comatose after you disrespected an adult, especially your parents.

I don't claim to know what caused such erratic behavior on our parent's part, but I think it might have been associated with the drugs they were using back then. In those days there was an excessive amount of Epsom Salt, Vaseline, Ex-Lax and rubbing alcohol being used. It was common knowledge that these items could cure everything from the common cold to cancer. Folks were even known to ingest castor oil and sugar because they believed the stuff would cure a sore throat. They also wrapped tight rags around their head to stop a headache. Chewing on a sassafras stick and drinking tea made from its roots was thought to improve vision. Man, all those home remedies had to do some serious damage to your brain cells!

After I spouted off to my mother, she grabbed a broom with full intentions of putting me in a state of time out. I made a rather hasty decision that would later prove to be a detriment to life and limb—I ran! I didn't run to Woodstock, I climbed a huge walnut tree in our front yard where I knew she could not possibly get to me. For a moment I was fairly confident that I had won this battle. And guess what? I was right! She never attempted to climb that huge walnut tree!

But, I did make another profound discovery. I learned that mothers know how to shell butter beans.

For all you youngsters and city slickers who don't have a clue what shelling beans is all about, let me explain. Butter beans grow on a vine and when they mature you take a large container (in our case it was a washtub) and pick or pull those butter beans off the vine. You then spend the rest of your life getting the beans out of their hull or shell. I was always told that this saves money, plus garden-grown butter beans are supposed to taste better than store bought. I was also informed of how proud I would be when winter came when we would all be sitting around the dinner table enjoying those hot, garden-grown butter beans. I never did figure all that out—I guess it was just another result of the castor oil and sugar.

I know you're just dying to know what back talking, climbing trees, and shelling butter beans has got in common with one another. My mother dragged that big washtub full of butter beans underneath that walnut tree where I had perched myself like a bird on a limb. She never said a word to me or even acknowledged that I was up there. She simply sat quietly shelling those butter beans and humming her favorite church hymns as she slowly worked on the task at hand. Finally, after about two hours, it seemed to me that my backside was beginning to graft itself to that tree limb. By then I figured she had forgotten all about what I had said and I decided to come down. With the confidence of victory I started my descent out of that walnut tree. Coming down wasn't too difficult except for the last step where you had to grab hold of a low limb, swing around where you were suspended in the air about three feet from the ground, then drop. Just as I made my swing, while still suspended from that limb, my dear old sainted mother took a peach tree switch that she had hidden out of sight and put her loving son in time out!

To this day every time I see a walnut tree, butter beans, or peach trees it brings tears to my eyes. Those kinds of bad life experiences can create some heavy phobias if you do not deal properly with them. To make matters worse, to this day I still don't like butter beans and I'm still not proud when winter comes!

Have you ever wondered why we think that time heals all wounds? Where did we get the notion that after a period of time the pain and hurt goes away? Fact is, it not only doesn't go away it gets worse. The hurts become so ingrained in our thinking that they become a part of us and grow right along with us as the years pass. I've met so many people over the years who are angry, bitter, and frustrated with life and they cannot figure out why. If you were to ask them for a logical explanation why they are so angry, most couldn't tell you. They are just mad as the devil himself and don't know why or who they are angry with.

But ask their spouse, their children, or their coworkers, and they can tell you. The fact is, it all started with a dumb mistake, a wrong word, or a simple misunderstanding. Whether intentional or accidental, don't you think it is time to come down out of the walnut tree? And though the descent may be painful, I'll assure you that the ground is a lot more stable and lots more comfortable! And I can also guarantee you something else: it is a lot better than castor oil and sugar!

Groovy, Man!

"Train up a child in the way he should go: and when he is
old, will not depart from it."
Proverbs 22:6

The 1960s and 70s teenagers growing up in Lick Skillet were not so different from other teens around the country. I've noticed that no matter what the geographic location, all teens go through that difficult time when they are attempting to discover where and how they fit into society. And if you happen to be parents then you understand. At this very moment there are thousands of borderline insane people in households across America cohabitating with these strange beings we call teenagers! Be afraid, be very afraid!

But while you're living with them, just remind yourself that we've all been there, done that, and your teen is probably no weirder than you were at that age! You may not realize it now but this is a special time in every family where the three C's prevail: chaos, confusion and counseling!

Being a teenager in every generation has its pitfalls, potholes, and dangers. One of these is the tendency of society to put its citizens under tremendous pressure to conform to what others generally accept as a way of life. Today we have the philosophical meanderings of the anti-God crowd. We have organizations that want to attack the values society has held sacred for generations. There are the politically correct who are attempting to force the majority to accept the will of the minority. Pressures, pressures, pressures! And sadly, if there happens to be that rare individual who does not necessarily agree with what the majority regards as normal, that person is usually regarded as strange, odd, or radical. Unfortunately, a conformist will usually go along with the crowds rather than run the risk of being labeled.

I am convinced that one of our life's biggest tragedies is this movement toward conformity, whether it is in government, in business, in our homes, social and civic activities, or even in church.

As a teenager I was one of those radical 1960s hippie types. I grew up listening to musical rock groups like the Beatles, the Dave Clark Five, the Beach Boys, and the ever-famous Sam the Sham and the Pharaohs. If you can remember those guys in their heyday, it reveals your age and probably your basic philosophy of life.

For those who didn't grow up in the Woodstock era, there was a popular saying: "Do your own thing." What this meant was "Be radical" or "Dare to be different." Sounds good, doesn't it? We were encouraged to be independent, free, and have that feeling of being our own person. Radicals were encouraging teens to be the round peg in a square hole, and not to fear being the odd piece in the puzzle of life. However, the only problem with that philosophy was no one was doing it. Oh, we thought we were! Even the leaders propagating that junk thought they were being non-conformists.

Everyone was conforming! We were all wearing bell-bottom pants, miniskirts, purple and yellow shirts, and sporting long hair. And we were all using words like peace, groovy, and dude. We were *all* using the same phrases like

Far-out! What's happening? and *Peace man!* while holding up two fingers in the form of a V. We didn't have enough sense to realize that Winston Churchill was doing the "V" thing long before the 1960 hippie crowd picked it up! In other words, everybody was yelling *independence* and *freedom* while at the same time doing what everybody else was doing—conforming to the crowd!

As a pastor I have noticed that the Christian community at large is also affected by the pressures to conform. The Bible makes it absolutely clear that we are not to conform to the standards established by the world. But despite clear biblical teachings to the contrary, we still buckle under the strain. The apostle Paul said, "And be not conformed to this world" (Romans 12:2).

Often, the idea of many as to what the church is or is not is determined more by what others *do* than by what the Bible teaches. Many Christians are more impressed with things that are popular than with what the New Testament instructs.

It might help us to remember that Jesus Christ is to be our example. He did not choose for Himself the easy route. He did not concern Himself with seeking popularity. And one thing is for certain, Jesus never gave much thought to being politically correct. He made it explicitly clear that His followers must leave behind the ways of the world and seek treasure in heaven. But by this statement He never intended us to be so heavenly minded that we are no earthly good. Followers of Jesus Christ are to be examples of what being a good citizen is. The Bible teaches that we are to walk in love for God and our fellowman, work consistently, and give an honest day's work as well as being ethical in our dealings with others.

If we ever hope to live a life that is pleasing to God we must conform, not to the ways of the world but to the teachings of Scripture. By conforming to the teachings and practices of Jesus Christ we actually end up being a non-conformist in the world. Are you aware that there is no instance in the Bible where the majority was ever right? I have always found this fact very interesting.

As parents, understand that your teenagers are simply feeling their way through life right now. I realize that this is a difficult time, but remember that your parents survived when you were going through this stuff! My best advice is to do your best to be patient with the green hair, baggy pants, tattoos, and body piercing. I understand that they may appear as though they got into a fight with a nail gun and lost. And I don't doubt that your teenage son looks like he tripped over his baggy pants and fell head first into a tackle box. But just understand that this too will pass! Just do your best to guide them in these formative years to be themselves and not a mini-caricature of someone else. Teach them to think for themselves, to seek and trust God through Jesus Christ in all they do, and to treat others like they would like to be treated. If you accomplish this you have fulfilled your parental mission. I don't know about you, but I think that is pretty groovy!

Winter Rafting

"My son, if sinners entice thee, consent thou not."
Proverbs 1:10

There is one winter day in 1964 that stands out vividly in my mind. It was on a Sunday afternoon when most of my relatives had gathered at my grandparents' house for a weekly traditional family meal. For some reason the winter of '64 was unusually wet as well as bitterly harsh. It was so cold that the river located near my grandparents' house was almost completely frozen. Notice I said *almost* frozen—a bit of information that will become extremely important later in the story.

Several of my cousins became bored of listening to all that adult chatter and decided to take a walk down to the river to get a closer look at the ice. The previous day snow had fallen and there was at least two inches on the ground. Many of our neighbors' water pipes had already frozen, thus making life generally miserable.

When my cousins got to the river's edge one noticed that the ice was only frozen approximately twenty feet out from both banks, leaving the main channel to flow freely. Immediately, the oldest suddenly experienced an overwhelming wave of super-intellect and put forth a tremendous idea, "Hey, let's all get on the ice, chip it away from the bank, and float it down the river like a raft!" (I'm not sure, but I think he's a brain surgeon now). All his fellow companions thought this was a great idea (must be genetic) and began looking for sticks, stones, or whatever primitive tools they could find and set to the task of chipping away at a large chunk of the ice. And guess what? It worked—for about ten feet! When brain-man and his fellow rocket scientists reached the channel, that ice raft did a complete flip in the middle of the river. Later my cousin's would privately testify that you haven't fully lived to your greatest potential until you have been dunked in ten feet of water from a huge ice raft during one of the coldest winter days on record. Add having to swim back to the bank, then walking back to my grandfather's house through the snow with your clothes completely soaked. (Note: In the South we discovered that wet snow will stick to you like glue and just keep collecting as long as you walk in it.) By the time they got back to the house they all looked like a cross between the Pillsbury Doughboy and the Michelin Man. It appeared as though my aunts were doing ice sculptures as they chipped away at those ice-laden clothes looking for some semblance of humanity underneath all that frozen snow turned ice. Believe me, when all was said and done (and I can testify that there was a lot said and done), that ice raft wasn't the only thing that flipped that day.

Have you ever had plans that flipped-flopped despite your best efforts? You plan, you research, you put all the principles in place but something unexpected happens and it all seems to blow up in your face. What are we to do in such situations? Cry? Whine? Run? Complain? Unfortunately, that's what most of us do. We live in a fast paced, instantaneous world. We have microwave ovens, remote control televisions, push-button this and push-button that. We live in a nation that has everything from instant on to instant pudding, which has led us to become a *no patience* society.

Of the few things I did learn at LSU (Lick Skillet University) one principle that was drilled into every student's thinking was "If it's worth doing, it's worth doing right!" And doing it right takes time, patience, and sometimes means doing it over and over again until you get it correct. Sometimes the best approach is not doing it at all! Believe me, it is a lot better *not* to allow others to talk you into doing something you may regret later.

I can certainly guarantee you one thing—the next time those cousins of mine went rafting they did so in July!

Playing Hooky

"Surely in vain the net is spread in the sight of any bird."
Proverbs 1:17

During my senior year of high school a friend and I decided that we would play hooky. At the time the thrill of skipping school seemed like a great idea. We planned to ride around in his customized 1953 Ford, play a game or two of billiards, and have a burger at one of the local hangouts. It sure was cool thinking how we would be having all that fun while our classmates would be bored stiff in history class.

Almost from the onset our well-planned strategy started going south, or in our case, north. In my excitement I overlooked the fact that we couldn't hang around Lick Skillet because my mother was the postmaster and knew every soul south of the Mason-Dixon Line. Okay, no problem; we'd just hurriedly head across the Tennessee state line, which unknowingly to us meant we were now guilty of interstate flight.

We hadn't traveled long before the next major miscalculation manifested itself. We hadn't anticipated driving so far and soon discovered that neither of us had enough money to feed the appetite of that gas guzzling Ford V8. Therefore, the little money we did have went into the gas tank, leaving us foodless, Coke-less, and virtually penniless, which now meant we were guilty of vagrancy. Suddenly the thrill of victory was becoming the agony of defeat. We ended up spending the entire day on the north side of Ardmore, Tennessee sitting in a state park under a big oak tree convinced that this was the longest day in the history of mankind.

The third huge incident of stupidity occurred the next day when we both agreed to sign each other's excuse note as if our parents had done it. Of course this action resulted in us now being guilty of forgery. In just a short twenty-four hour span, we both went from high school seniors to Machine Gun Kelly and Baby Face Nelson.

Looking back on that incident I realized this is where I learned the truth of, "But if ye will not do so, behold, ye have sinned against the Lord: and be sure your sin will find you out" (Numbers 32:23). The truth of this verse was certainly illustrated in a vivid way for my companion and me. For example, how was I to know that Mr. Maze, a farmer who knew us both, would be traveling to a cattle auction in Ardmore and spot us sitting in that state park? And another thing: What in the world possessed our history teacher to give a quiz that Friday, after we had bribed a buddy to answer to our names when the teacher called the class attendance roll? And what earthly reason did our school principal have for calling my mother at the post office to verify that forged excuse?

We both knew we needed to come up with something quick to justify our actions. So, being the model detainees that we were, we did what any red-blooded American criminals would do when faced with a similar situation—we pleaded temporary insanity.

That pitiful pleading and begging almost worked! At

least we didn't get expelled for three days, which is what our principal wanted to do. Instead, he compromised after he learned that our parents agreed to take care of the situation themselves. We spent the next several days writing 1,000 word themes on why you shouldn't skip school. We listened to lecture after lecture about how we were ruining our lives, how irresponsible we were, and how we were going to end up in juvenile detention for life. The pastor of our church even went further—he told us that if we didn't straighten up we both might go to hell.

Someone once said concerning sinful deeds, "You may not get caught, but you'll never get away!" My friend and I can both testify that more likely than not, not only will you *not* get away, but you'll also *be* caught.

Making dumb choices can be costly. We need to remember that the world is full of people like Mr. Maze, school principals, concerned parents, and nosey neighbors who all feel it is their civic responsibility to turn you in. But more importantly our Father in heaven loves us enough that He is not about to let you get away with willful sin. By the way, have you played spiritual hooky lately?

Drag Racin' Grandpa

"The glory of young men is their strength:
and the beauty of old men is the grey head."
Proverbs 20:29

My maternal grandfather was quite a character, to say the least! He was not only my grandfather, but also my friend. He lived his entire life working in construction and could build anything from a birdhouse to a skyscraper. He was also probably the most opinionated man I have ever met; he would argue with a stop sign. One of his favorite pastimes was to sit in Al's Barber Shop with a group of other hard-headed, likeminded old men and together they would attempt to settle all the world's problems. Primarily, it ended up being nothing more than a debate between the Democrats and the Republicans, the Baptists and the Church of Christ, and the Auburn Tigers and Alabama Crimson Tide football teams. They would fuss, fume, and fight and would usually all leave mad at each other until the next week when they would meet to do it all over again. I said to him one day after an argument, "You are the most hard-headed, stubborn person I have ever met!" To which he politely smiled and said, "Son, you don't know your grandmother very well do you?"

There was one incident that involved my grandfather and me that nearly got both of us kicked out of the family. When I turned eighteen, I purchased my first automobile, a 1966 Ford Fairlane GT with the largest engine I could cram under the hood. You have to understand that in Lick Skillet, if you did not have a fast car you were socially left out of the loop. Every Saturday night the locals would gather at the cotton gin parking lot for a pre-race meeting so we could prove who had the fastest car. We called it the skillet strip, but in reality it was a paved two-lane stretch on Butter and Egg Road that ran between two country grocery stores. It was there that we would race down the quarter-mile strip. Actually, it was nothing more than a yellow starting line and a white finish line someone had painted approximately a quarter mile apart.

I was so proud of that hotrod Ford and I thought it could outrun a long-distance telephone call. Somehow, after I purchased that car, I just knew I was going to be the fastest redneck in the Skillet. I had dreams of being the next Butter and Egg Road drag racing champion. I was going to be the Yahoo of LSU (Lick Skillet University) when the next race was scheduled and I could hardly wait.

Sadly, it didn't take me long to discover that my little Ford wasn't the only bad boy on the block. In one humiliating, embarrassing, and disgusting moment all my dreams of being crowned the fastest streak in the Skillet disappeared before my eyes. And guess who taught me that lesson? You guessed it, my dear old granddaddy!

It all began on my way to work one Monday morning as I was cruising along looking as cool as any 125 pound, longhaired, country bumpkin driving a 1966 Ford Fairlane GT could. I had all the windows down and was listening to my favorite singing group, Credence Clearwater Revival singing, "Do, do, do, looking out my back door!" That's when I spied him traveling south on Highway 231 heading to Huntsville. He was looking as cool as any 70-year-old blue-haired man could (the hair dye just didn't work for him). He was minding his own business, listening to Johnny Cash singing "Ring of Fire" on the 8-track. I pulled alongside of my grandfather's car and gave him *the look!* You need to understand that he was also a fan of large engine automobiles and was the proud owner of an old four-door 65 Chevrolet Impala with a 396 cubic inch engine crammed under the hood. And just as that old geezer got beside me he returned *the look* and I knew right away what that meant. He slammed the accelerator to the floor on that old Impala just about the very instant that I punched my little Ford. We came off the hill in Meridianville side by side in a dead heat. Three miles later as we reached Huntsville city limits, we were hitting speeds of over 100 miles per hour. We were side by side with not one of us wanting to give in to the other. Finally, I had to back off; the last time I saw that crazy old man that day he was looking at me in his rearview mirror and laughing at me.

I'm certainly not advocating what we did was a good thing. We broke the law and endangered lives and both should have been arrested and fined. But I do want to make a point by posing a question: what makes a person old? Is it age, aches and pains, retirement, social security? I imagine these things are a result of aging, but would you entertain the possibility just for a moment that getting old might be a state of mind? When does a person get old? Is there some magic number we reach that automatically declares a person elderly?

These are sobering questions that I'm afraid most of us are either too tired or too frightened to ask. It is amazing that Americans spend billions of dollars each year on sprays, creams, pills, exercise equipment, facelifts, plastic surgeries, and for what? So we can look and feel young again. Ever wonder if maybe we are looking for youth in all the wrong places?

Do you think it is an accident that people get old when they stop playing? When we were children we played constantly and were continually looking for new things to do and adventures to enjoy. When did we lose our sense of wonder? When did we lose the fascination of a butterfly or the mystery of what makes birds fly? Do you still wonder why a giraffe's neck is so long or why God made the duck-billed platypus? Did we get all the answers somewhere along the line and thus fulfill all our fascinations and curiosities? Or did we simply convince ourselves that our time on earth is limited and there are no adventures to have, no more worlds to conquer, no new things to explore?

I have two granddaughters of my own: a five-year-old and a two-year-old. Since their birth, both those girls have renewed my sense of wonder and fascination with the world around me. Through their eyes I have once again seen the rainbow in a different light. Suddenly pecans, grasshoppers, different colored leaves, rocks, kittens, and puppies have a peculiar fascination that I had not noticed in a long time. And you know something? I'm not sure, but I think I'm getting younger again. Without realizing it, my granddaughters are helping me appreciate God's wonderful creation in ways that I haven't in years. Want to know something else? It feels really, really good!

Is your life one of loneliness, despair, and filled with doom and gloom? Come on, give it a whirl and reclaim your sense of wonder. You may discover that if you refocus outwardly it just may change you inwardly!

Kidney Stones

"As he that bindeth a stone in a sling,
so is he that giveth honour to a fool."
Proverbs 26:8

A s you read this chapter I am lying in a bed suffering from a kidney stone attack. As I lie here with my body and brain saturated with Demerol and morphine, I am studying my Bible, seeking answers to my dilemma. After an in-depth exegesis I have come to some definite conclusions concerning trials and tribulations.

Did you know that an illness could actually be scripturally enlightening? Before you call the *God Squad* to have me excommunicated, please hear me out. Ever since 1975 I have been plagued (a better word might be cursed) with developing kidney stones very rapidly. They have actually been a way of life for me for nearly thirty years. I have had so many that I'm saving every stone I pass so I can have a tombstone constructed once they kill me. As a matter of fact, I am convinced (both through experience, as well as an in-depth study of the Scriptures) that the apostle Paul's thorn in the flesh (2 Corinthians 12:7) was no doubt a kidney stone. I realize that theologians have speculated for years what his thorn was so I want to assert my kidney stone hypothesis. How did I arrive at such a miraculous conclusion, you may ask? It was through simple theological and expositional principles deducted through grammatical and doctrinal homiletical interpretation based solely upon an orthodox and pre-millennial view. There! It is really not that complicated when you understand how I arrived at my conclusions.

Okay, now that that's out of the way, back to my interpretation. In verse 8 we see Paul pleading and begging. He writes, "For this thing I besought the Lord thrice, that it might depart from me" (2 Corinthians 12:8).

If you have ever had a kidney stone you will find yourself doing a lot of beseeching and lots of pleading and begging. "Please unlock the car door and let me jump out!" Or, "Please doctor, just go ahead and shoot me!" "Please Mr. X-ray technician, drop that machine on my head and knock me out!" Yes, pleading and begging are a natural result of kidney stones.

The second piece of evidence that indicates that Paul suffered from kidney stones is again found in verse 8. Notice that Paul is asking for *it* to depart. Departing has a two-fold possibility. If you cross reference 2 Corinthians 12 with Philippians 1:23, you find these words, "For I am in a strait betwixt the two, having a desire to depart... which is far better." This is Paul's earnest desire to die! You had better believe that a desire to die on the part of one with a kidney stone is a natural part of the torturous, unrelenting process of pain and agony. But, on the other hand, this could also mean a desire for the kidney stone to depart (which is far better) and be at rest. No doubt about it, Paul is *pleading* for it to *depart,* which is great evidence that his problem was a kidney stone.

Okay, there also might be a third conclusion. There is also associated with a kidney stone a touch of insanity. The excruciating pain definitely causes you to do and say things that others around you don't understand. Believe me, kidney stones have a tendency to readjust your attitude toward others. For example, let's imagine that you are sitting in the hospital emergency room waiting for the doctors to finally get to you. During this time, most who suffer from kidney stones will usually begin screaming and pleading for it to *depart*. Naturally, you will always have those concerned people around you who will ask very intelligent questions like, "Does it hurt?" To which you respond calmly and Christian-like, "No, I'm just down here wallowing on the floor checking out the underside of these chairs for bubblegum." It never fails that you will hear some woman say, "You know, having a baby actually hurts *worse!*" To which you remember you're a Christian and you respond with a biblical answer like the apostle Paul did in 1 Corinthians 14:9, "So likewise ye, except ye utter by the tongue words easy to be understood, how shall it be known what is spoken? For ye shall speak into the air" (KJV).

Or you could get in the flesh and say, "Great, I hear the hospital is giving the pain prize, and guess what, I'm the winner!" But as Christians we realize we can't respond like that, so we need to be biblical about it and simply give a spiritual reply like, "Answer not a fool according to his folly, lest thou also be like unto him" (Proverbs 26:4).

But notice how Paul responded, "Therefore I take pleasure in infirmities" (2 Corinthians 12:10). Do you realize what he is saying? He's actually saying, "I like it, give me more, this makes me strong!" If this is a kidney stone (and I believe it is) either one of two things has happened here. Either he is in so much pain that he is about to lose consciousness and does not realize what he is saying, or else his morphine pump has just kicked in.

Speaking of morphine pumps, I think mine just kicked in also. Wow, this stuff sure does funny things to your head. For one thing it makes you say things that others seem to find humorous. Also, morphine has a tendency to cause authors like me to write ridiculous stuff like this chapter. One thing is for certain, kidney stones are sure bad news. Did you know that morphine also affects your biblical interpretations and causes you to become theologically twisted? Hey, I'll bet you didn't know that! How about if I just talk to you in the next chapter after my head clears?

Dream Machine

"A good name is rather to be chosen than great riches, and
loving favour rather than silver and gold."
Proverbs 22:1

When I was fourteen years of age my dad purchased
the most beautiful motorcycle I had ever seen. It was
a 1964 Honda 305 "Dream" edition that was completely
decked to the hilt with windshield, crash bars, saddlebags,
and lights galore. For a fourteen-year-old boy who already
had a love affair with motorcycles, this was about as close to
heaven as one could get without actually dying. My
emotions were off the charts and I never imagined anything
could ever get any better than this. A few of my friends
owned motorcycles, but those were mainly little single-
cylinder Yamahas, a few Hondas, and dirt bikes, but none
had anything close to my 305 Dream.

One Sunday afternoon a group of us decided to meet after
church and spend the afternoon cruising the countryside. In
the 1960s there wasn't as much traffic as today; for the most
part we had the road to ourselves except for an occasional
automobile or farm tractor. My friends and I enjoyed every
mile as we spent the entire afternoon riding our bikes.

But all good things must end, so at approximately 4:00 p.m. we headed for home so we would not be late for church services, which began in an hour. Attending church was a priority in the Fanning household and I realized that my parents would never tolerate me missing church because of a motorcycle ride.

As soon as I left the group I started for home. It was at this very moment that I made one of stupidest, most hair-brained decisions that I have regretted to this day. Instead of turning right when I pulled out of my friend's driveway and heading straight home, I decided to turn left and take the long route so I could get in just a little more riding time before church. The problem was that I underestimated the mileage difference in the two routes and soon figured that I was going to be late getting home. I was horrified at the thought of my parents waiting on me and I knew they would be extremely upset and probably ground me for at least a month. I decided to speed up, assuming that if I hurried, I might just make it and no one would ever know what I had done.

As I came around a curve I immediately found myself staring down a steep hill that appeared to be at least three miles in length. That is when I made the dumb decision to twist the throttle on that Honda Dream. Before I realized it the speedometer was pegging close to 100 mph. Approximately halfway down the hill I spotted an automobile heading toward me in the other lane. I immediately decided to slow down, but when you are a novice traveling at over 100 mph you soon discover that traveling from point A to point B is quicker than you anticipate. It didn't take me long to figure out that I was not going to get slowed down nearly enough, and so I decided to keep moving at my current speed.

Actually, it proved not to make much difference anyway because just as I got even with that automobile I realized whom I had met. It was my dad (who knew me better than I knew myself and figured that I had taken that long route home) out searching for me to make sure I was not in an accident. When I hadn't arrived home my parents had called my friend's house and were informed of the time I had left heading for home.

As soon as I passed my dad's old 1956 Chevrolet I immediately began to experience panic attacks, horror, dysentery, migraine headaches, as well as entertain serious thoughts of suicide. I knew that once I arrived home my life as I had always known it was either going to change or end. I also realized that all the church services and all the spiritual repenting in heaven and on earth were not going to make this situation go away.

When I finally arrived at home my father did something that has baffled me all these years. As I pulled that little Honda into our driveway I noticed that my dad's car was immediately behind me. He got out of his car, walked over to the motorcycle, and simply pulled the key out of the ignition. He never uttered a word as he put that key in his pocket and got back into his car. My mother and two sisters came out of the house and we all joined him in the car and headed for church. During the entire trip to church and back home my dad never said anything about the incident.

The next day everything seemed to be normal around our house. That morning my family went through their regular routines of getting ready for school and work. Still, there was not one word spoken about the events of the previous day. It was the weirdest thing I had ever experienced because I was fully expecting the hammer to fall on me and was confused why it hadn't. But somehow I had this perpetual nauseous feeling that judgment day was coming. I knew there was going to be some heavy retribution, I just didn't know when or how - until I got home that afternoon.

I had ridden the school bus home that evening and when the bus stopped at our house I noticed my dad standing next to my motorcycle talking to the pastor of our church. I was somewhat confused and wondered why the preacher would be the least bit interested in looking at my motorcycle. I immediately thought, "Okay, now I know what's going to happen. Dad's turned this situation over to the preacher, and he's going to give me a long lecture on being responsible." But that's not what happened. Just as I walked over to where they were standing I saw our pastor write my dad a check. My dad then handed the pastor a pink slip of paper and I watched as both men signed it. It was then that I understood what had happened. My dad had just sold my motorcycle to the pastor of our church!

I didn't know what to say and just decided that the best thing for me to do was keep silent. But my heart was broken as I watched the pastor's son mount that beautiful motorcycle and ride off with his dad following along close behind. My father and I stood beside each other as they left and we watched them until they were out of sight. At this point my dad turned and looked at me and simply said, "Boy, don't you ever bring up the subject of that motorcycle again!" And with that, he simply walked away.

I didn't have to bring it up. There was no reason to ask why because I knew why. My dad had given me the best gift possible and I had been irresponsible and knew fully that I had let my father down.

I am now in my fifties and my father passed away in February of 1999. Over the years he and I talked about a lot of things, especially during those special conversations we had in the weeks prior to his death. But you know, out of all those conversations that motorcycle incident was never mentioned!

Over the years I have thought about that motorcycle situation many times and have come to some conclusions. I have often considered how our heavenly Father has given us the best gift possible, namely His own Son, Jesus Christ, to die on a cross to obtain for us eternal life. But more often than not in my daily relationship with Him I have in all probability repeated this same irresponsible motorcycle situation over and over. It may manifest itself in different ways, but the principle is the same. Far too many times I have been irresponsible, unthankful, and have misused His gift of grace as a license to do things I know I shouldn't.

Before you face the inevitable temptation to do something that you know is wrong, why not make a commitment *now* to think before you act. Make up your mind beforehand that you will do your best to do the right thing. Failure to do so could result in God pulling the keys to some of the best blessings you'll ever experience. Make sure you do not miss out!

Where the Rubber Meets the Road

"Whoso keepeth his mouth and his tongue keepeth
his soul from troubles."
Proverbs 21:23

A s a pastor, the stresses and strains of ministry sometimes get to be a bit overwhelming. If ministers (as
well as other high-stress professions) do not have some
avenue of release, then all that mental, physical, emotional,
and spiritual pressure will eventually catch up to you.

For me, I have been driving eighteen-wheel trucks for
many years. No big deal. It is just something that I enjoy
doing occasionally and it gives me an opportunity to get
away from daily pressures and enjoy the open road. I guess
it is the leftover remnants of that freedom thing from my
late 1960s teenage past.

On one of these *freedom* runs I was dispatched from the
home trucking terminal with a load of goods that was to be
delivered to a large warehouse in rural south Mississippi. At
the time I thought my terminal dispatcher was very specific
in his instructions; he even gave me a computer printout

detailing my route. With the destination set and the truck ready, all I had to do was follow instructions, right? Right! So how did I make a wrong turn that placed me on a two-lane Mississippi country road with no place large enough to turn around that huge truck? How did I make such a major miscalculation that caused the scheduled delivery time to be delayed for almost two hours? What possibly could have caused such a blunder that an elderly woman standing next to the road's edge checking her mailbox would call me mean and disgusting things? Okay, I've had time to evaluate and upon careful analysis I think I understand how all that happened.

From childhood, my mind has had a tendency to drift. It is a serious mental problem referred to as A.D.D or, in my case, *Affirmed Dufus Damage.* That's right! A competent counselor diagnosed me with the disease and I was informed that I inherited this trait from my parents due to a faulty genetic makeup. You just don't know what a relief it is to know that you are no longer responsible for any mistakes or blunders you may make. In other words, I am definitely considered certified by the U.S. government and have a card to prove it. Over the years I have learned not to give my personal mistakes much thought because I know what the problem is and have a good excuse for being irresponsible.

Therefore, I've decided that the dispatcher wasn't clear in his directions. Upon careful reflection, I feel my personal interpretation of his otherwise faulty instructions was a legitimate excuse for the error (and I told him so!). Oh, and one more thing: I don't know why I was sent to that place anyway. It appears to me that anyone with a brain should have known better than to build a warehouse in the rural countryside of south Mississippi!

Now wait a moment. Does the above scenario sound vaguely familiar? Are you one of those individuals who constantly searches for excuses to explain or hide your mistakes? Why is it that we are so prideful that we cannot admit it when we do something wrong? Isn't it unfortunate that we live in a pass-the-buck society and consistently play the blame game when it comes to personal errors?

That is bad enough when we do this with our fellow-man, but it is a spiritual disaster in the making if we try this with God. Sadly, all of us from time to time make the same error in our relationship with Him as I did on that trucking trip. Why is it that God has given us specific and clear instructions in His Word and yet we ignore or misinterpret them? Why do we always have to do the old buck passing trick, making excuses for our sins and mistakes? Jesus knows we are going to mess up from time to time. That is why He died on the cross, to provide us with the privilege of acknowledging our sin, seeking His forgiveness, and inviting Him into our lives. Simple, huh?

But, we can choose to continue making excuses for our sins and bad behavior if we desire to do so. Just make sure that you understand that one day, when you die and stand in judgment, all your excuses will go about as far with God as mine did with the dispatcher.

Unfounded Fears

"Bread of deceit is sweet to a man; but afterwards his
mouth shall be filled with gravel."
Proverbs 20:17

I am getting older and I can hardly believe that I am now
in my 50s. When I shared that fact with a childhood
friend recently I said, "Man, can you believe we are now
middle-aged?" To which he responded, "Middle-aged?
Come on, just how many people do you know who actually
live to be one hundred?"

I have discovered that this getting older thing has a
tendency to teach you some things about life. Over the years
I've witnessed some really scary moments that were enough
to gray anyone's hair at an early age.

I have also learned that ninety percent of all the things
that I worried about when I was younger never transpired.
Let me share with you some examples of what I mean....

Do you remember or at least have heard of the Orson
Wells fiasco of 1938? It was Halloween night when Wells
began to broadcast his now famous *War of the Worlds* drama.
It was a fiction thriller meant solely for the entertainment of
the audience, or so that was his intention. But the invention

of radio was relatively new and since many in the audience either tuned in late or simply did not hear the announcement at the beginning of his broadcast that this was only a play, many believed it was a real event. Wells convinced listeners that that a "huge flaming object' had fallen on a farm near Grovers Mill, New Jersey and alien Martians were presently combing the New Jersey countryside looking for earthlings and destroying everything in their path. Members of the audience sat on the edge of their collective seats as actors portrayed news announcers and officials anyone would have expected to hear in a news report. Panic ran rampant as hundreds sat terrified, glued to their radios fully believing the earth was being invaded. Hundreds more left their homes and personal belongings as they jammed the roadways leading out of the cities. Why? Because Orson Wells had successfully tapped into the subconscious fears of an entire nation and convinced them the end was near. Instead of hearing the truth, they opted for the fantasy and believed the lie even though the broadcast contained a number of explanations that it was only a radio play.

Another situation that struck fear into the hearts of an entire nation occurred in the early 1960s when a little bald-headed man named Nikita Khrushchev, then leader of Soviet Russia, in a speech promised America, "We will bury you!" This is the same Nikita Khrushchev who went nose to nose with President John F. Kennedy in the now-famous Cuban Missile Crisis.

It was a frightening time in our history when the United States and Russia were locked in a nuclear arms race and both countries were building bombs faster than we had places to put them.

We were all convinced that the Russians were coming and that they were going to bury us. Barbed wire and military tanks actually lined the shores and beaches of the Florida coastline and the American military was placed on high alert in case we were attacked.

This fear caused us to do some really weird things—like have nuclear attack drills at school. All the students at LSU (Lick Skillet University) were herded into the hallways where we would have to sit against the wall with a book over our head. You know, like if a nuclear bomb exploded on Butter and Egg Road that book over your head was supposed to save your life? Yeah, right! Even as an eleven year old I knew better than to believe that!

Contractors fed off these ridiculous fears and made millions selling and building nuclear bomb shelters in people's backyards. The military surplus stores couldn't keep up with orders for air masks and other life-saving paraphernalia. Everybody was purchasing guns and taking personal defense courses. Why? Because the Russians were coming, the Russians were coming!

Apparently, it never crossed anyone's mind to stop for a moment, breathe deeply and simply ask, "Okay, how does sitting in a hallway at LSU with a book over my head protect me from a nuclear attack?" Or, "If I go into that bomb shelter located in my backyard during a nuclear attack, will I have enough milk and bread to survive for the next one hundred years when it is finally safe enough for me to come out after the radiation level decreases?" The question that is probably most important: "Does a nuclear attack truly sound like a freight train?" Let me see, if this was a television game show I believe the correct response would be, "What is NO!"

Why do we do the dumb things we do? Remember Y2K? You do remember January 2000, don't you? That was the year of the Y2K scare, when all the computers were supposed to crash and life as we now know it would end. We were told that we needed to stock up on supplies so we could all survive the big bang. Airplanes would fall out of the sky, nuclear warheads would be unleashed on the world, the space shuttle would be stranded in outer space, banks would lose all their records and we'd all be financially ruined. We would lose our homes, our children, our pets. And we would all have to run out at 11:30 p.m. and buy milk and bread before it was too late. Ahhhh!

And what happened? Nothing! We all sat around the room, waiting anxiously for the clock to reach midnight so we could watch the computer explode. January 1 came and went and not a thing happened. There we were with all that milk and bread, stored supplies, and dumbfounded looks on our faces. We also discovered that weird sound we thought was coming from the computer was indeed a passing freight train.

Why do we do such silly things? Because most people live their entire life spiritually, emotionally, and mentally deceived. They live in a virtual twilight zone of their own making, a fantasy world of deception and half-truths. Then, when the incredible comes along, they will opt for the lie every time.

Did you know this has been a trick of Satan for centuries? If he can get us to chase our tails round and round, he knows we do not have much time to do anything else constructive. Remember what I said at the beginning of this chapter? Ninety percent of all the things I worried about never happened. Don't spend your life living in fear and intimidation, there is not that much milk and bread around! Resolve now not to be one of those who arrive at the end of life's road only to discover that you allowed irrational people with irrational fears prevent you from living a full life.

The Good Old Days

"Boast not thyself of tomorrow; for thou knowest not
what a day may bring forth."
Proverbs 27:1

How many times have you heard someone refer to the past as the good old days? I recently had a conversation with an elderly man who made that remark after he had just finished reminiscing about some cherished memory from his childhood. Later, as I reflected on what he had said, I got to thinking about "the good old days."

My childhood days were simple and carefree, but at the same time those days were tough and ones that I do not desire to repeat. Those were the days when my dad would wake us up at dawn for breakfast so we could work the cotton fields, dragging a cotton sack across 100-acre fields. Wonderful days when the sky was blue and the birds were singing, your hands and knees were bleeding, your back was hurting... just being out in God's world enjoying the creation (you've got to get a little spiritual). How I relish those happy times when it was 105 degrees in the shade and I was soaked from the morning dew until about 1:00 in the afternoon before I finally dried out. In those days I looked forward to school because it meant the end of picking cotton, pulling corn, or putting up hay. Oh how I long for the days when I could stick a pitchfork through my foot and Mother would wash it out with Epsom Salt, Clorox, rubbing alcohol, kerosene, tractor fuel, or whatever else she could find to kill the germs (and kill me in the process... as if the pitchfork through the foot wasn't enough!). She would then wrap the injury with a discarded bed sheet and give great advice like, "We'll clean it out again when we come in from the fields for lunch!" I just cherish the thought of winter days when my dad would tack burlap seed bags and cardboard over the holes and cracks in our house to keep the winter wind out. I hold dear the times when our family would bond around a coal-burning heater because the only place it was above thirty-two degrees was within a five-foot radius of the stove. And the thought of tracking to the well with metal buckets to get our daily water supply or walking across the yard to the outhouse still brings "jolly bumps" to my spine. Oh yes, the good old days!

It takes some honest mental evaluations to see that our "good old days" may be the ones we are living right now. The fact is that most of the stuff we remember may have some ring of truth to it, but I've noticed that for many we have a tendency to downplay the negative memories and inflate the positive ones. I suppose that in some ways living in the past helps us cope with the difficult circumstances we face in the present. For some unknown reason our minds want to recreate a perfect past with no problems.

Several years ago I knew of a man whose wife literally hung on his casket after he died and sobbed her heart out and told everyone what a great man and husband he was. The truth was he left her for a younger woman, was abusive to their children, and drank himself to death.

In some situations it is okay to have a selective memory if it helps us deal with bad past circumstances or preserves our present sanity. I feel that where we get into trouble is when a false recreated past tarnishes the reality of the here and now. As a pastor and conference speaker it never fails when I go to some church to speak or teach that someone will walk up and begin relating to me the glory days of their church. They remember when some famous pastor preached a revival and people were hanging in the windows and sitting around the pulpit because it was so crowded. They will sing the praises of their former pastors and tell you what a saint he was. They remember all the dinners on the ground and the great fellowships on Sunday nights and how they all loved each other through thick and thin.

The truth is, yes there were crowds and yes they had great pastors. But what they forgot to mention was that their former pastor was under constant pressure from meeting the needs of his congregation. They conveniently forgot to mention the troubled business meetings where irreparable damage was done and the church down the street is a result of the split. They omit the part about unfounded accusations hurled at fellow church members, where reputations were ruined and lives shattered.

Sitting here thinking about all of this reminds me of a passage of Scripture that deals with the story of Moses when he was in the process of leading the children of Israel from Egyptian slavery to the Promised Land. It says, "And the whole congregation of the children of Israel murmured against Moses and Aaron in the wilderness: And the children of Israel said unto them, Would to God we had died by the hand of the Lord in the land of Egypt, [do not miss this part] when we sat by the flesh pots, and when we did eat bread to the full; for ye have brought us forth into this wilderness, to kill this whole assembly with hunger" (Exodus 16:2–3).

Take your Bible and go back to that passage and read the background of the real reason why they were in the wilderness. They omitted the part about the harsh taskmasters with their whips. They forgot about the long, hard days working in the hot sun in Pharaoh's brick pits. In other words, the hard life of the present caused their minds to recreate a fictionalized heavenly past where there were no problems.

It is okay to reminisce about the good old days every now and then; if you feel you must reminisce to make sense of the present. But please, whatever you do, don't allow a reinvented past to soil your present or muddy your future. It is very possible that you are living your best days on earth right now. And remember something else: if you know Jesus Christ as your personal Savior, your best days *are* still ahead!

Responsibility Learned on the Tracks

"Be not wise in thine own eyes: fear the Lord,
and depart from evil."
Proverbs 3:7

When our children were growing up my wife and I did our best to teach them right from wrong. We were diligent in our efforts to teach the meaning of responsibility, hard work, and the value of keeping your word and being a person of character and integrity. Were we successful? Yes, even though we had our moments.

Both our children are now grown and making their own way through life. Our daughter is married; she and her husband stay busy raising two daughters. Our son is a home-owner and has a career as a draftsman with a local company. Both learned their life lessons well, and my wife and I are proud of how they both matured into responsible adults.

But even today there are those times when some of those *moments* we did not know about slip out—as a parent, you recognize you may not have known as much as you thought concerning your kid's activities. An example: recently, my wife and I went to visit her parents and our son decided to ride along with us (gas prices).

On the way, our son sent up a red flag in response to a comment I made as we crossed a railroad track. I casually said, "I sure am glad the railroad finally put up those flashing barricades." To which my son made an off-the-cuff comment that went something like, "Did you know that you can go about a quarter of a mile up the track and with a small piece of electrical wire cause the barricade arms to go up and down and the lights to flash?" I looked over at my wife; she looked at me and in tandem responded, "How do you know that?" Shrugging his shoulders he simply responded, "Oh, there are just some things you know!"

Hmmmm. For me the ultimate question is, did he learn how to short-circuit railroad barricades by reading that information in a book or did that bit of knowledge come by experience? Don't tell me! I don't really want to know!

I have a question: before you make a choice to do something, do you consider the consequences of that decision? I would probably say that most of us do not. But, if you are a Christian that is a question each of us should be asking ourselves every time we are faced with a decision.

Let's be honest, we have all made dumb decisions and done dim-witted things. You may not like admitting it, but you have. The question is, how did you respond? Did you make excuses, blame others, or simply ignore it and act as though nothing happened? I feel that the bottom-line question for all of us ought to be: "Is Jesus Christ worthy of our obedience and has there ever been a time where we made a conscious decision to follow Him in all we do?"

We all need to understand that there will be those times when we stumble and fall. But when we resolve in our heart to be obedient to God, that commitment will strengthen our resolve to follow Him when temptations to do wrong come our way.

Has there ever been a time in your life when you've messed up and done things you know you shouldn't have done? Then seek God's forgiveness and get on with your life. But more importantly, has there ever been a time when you made a personal commitment to obey God in all areas of your life? If the answer is *no*, then why not make that decision to do so today? After all, we don't need a stroll up the railroad track of life with a roll of electrical wire to know if something is a sin. Right, son?

Just Trust Me

"Trust in the Lord with all thine heart; and lean not unto
thine own understanding."
Proverbs 3:5

During the fall of 1970 some of my friends invited me to
go quail hunting. That was fine except that there was
one guy who had never hunted before but he insisted on
coming along. I know, I know. Common sense tells you that
it is unsafe to hunt with someone who is unfamiliar with
gun safety, but I decided to go along anyway.

The day came for the big hunt and surprisingly everybody arrived on time. My novice friend was the last to arrive
and when he got out of his car we beheld the most ridiculous
sight we'd ever seen. He'd obviously made a trip to the local
sporting goods store because he was dressed in the ugliest
camouflage hunting suit I had ever seen. It was a green-
splotched coat with matching pants, heavy military boots,
and a bright orange hat to complete his absurd ensemble. He
had also purchased a brand new Browning 16-gauge auto-
matic shotgun, complete with its own carrying case. He
looked like a cross between Rambo and a neon light as he
stood there looking at us with that ridiculous grin.

On our hunt we walked and walked and didn't see the first quail. I was relieved because I was still apprehensive about a neon Rambo carrying a loaded gun! However, for Rambo it was really frustrating because he was just itching to fire that new shotgun at something. Finally, he said to one of my buddies, "If you will pitch your hat in the air and let me shoot at it, then I'll let you shoot at mine." After a bit of discussion my best friend finally agreed and threw his hat into the air. Neon Rambo took his best shot and missed it by a mile. At that, Rambo started walking off and my best friend was hot on his heels reminding him of the deal they'd made. He argued his case as if he were standing before a judge. Finally, my buddy suggested a compromise, "Okay, you throw it into the air and I promise I won't hit it. Just trust me!"

Anyone who knew my friend very well knew that *just trust me* was the beginning of the end. After much persuasion Rambo finally threw his neon hat into the air. My friend aimed his gun and tracked it as it arched its way though the sky. Then, just as that hat landed solidly on the ground he pulled the trigger and buried it about three inches into the dirt! I never laughed so hard as when I watched Rambo dig up that goofy hat while simultaneously pouring buckshot and gunpowder onto the ground. In my mind's eye I can still see him as he stomped, fumed, and angrily huffed away with a smoky blue haze swirling wildly around the shot-up hat sitting on his head.

For me, every time I hear someone use the phrase "Just trust me" I am reminded of the fact that those famous last words, more often than not, lead to major disappointments. How many times did we place our trust in people who ended up letting us down? Maybe it was a friend who betrayed a trust, a business deal where you were taken advantage of, or even a relative who benefited by unscrupulous means from an inheritance. We could go on and on with situations that cause people to lose faith in the face of the term *just trust me!*

Do you realize that trust is at the heart of our relationship with Christ? The Scriptures admonish us to, "Trust in the Lord with all thine heart; and lean not unto thine own understanding. In all thy ways acknowledge him and he shall direct thy paths" (Proverbs 3:5–6).

Our responsibility is to trust, and the Lord's responsibility is to guide us in the way He'd have us go. When the God of the universe is the one saying *"Just trust me"* you can be assured that He won't shoot you down... no matter how ugly your hat!

The July 4th Incident

"Discretion shall preserve thee, understanding
shall keep thee."
Proverbs 2:11

Have you ever done anything that was really, really dim-witted? I don't mean those late night teen pranks when you put cow manure in a paper bag and placed it on the school principal's doorstep, set it afire then watched him stomp it out with his bare feet after you rang his doorbell.

Or how about the time you put that garden snake in an old purse and meticulously placed it in the road where some poor fortune seeker stopped, grabbed it, and hurriedly drove away only to abandon his car at 40 mph?

And I know you remember that day when you randomly choose a name in the telephone book, called them and asked, "Is your refrigerator running?" And when they affirmed that it was indeed running you responded, "Well, you better go catch it because it just passed by my house!"

Then there was that time—okay, okay—now that you are thoroughly under conviction, let me get to my story and point.

One Fourth of July in the summer of '65 some of my friends and I gathered down at the river that was used as the

153

neighborhood swimming hole. Somewhere in our conversation one of my friends (whose father happened to be a local farmer) said, "We've been clearing land with dynamite and I have two sticks in the trunk of my car!" Of course we all accused him of lying which naturally forced him to prove it. So he went to his car, raised the trunk and, sure enough, produced two sticks of dynamite along with the fuses and blasting caps. I can't begin to tell you how impressed we all were. Immediately the sight of those explosives inspired our peanut-sized minds to ponder what we might do with it. Finally one guy asked, "What do you guys think would happen if we threw a stick in the river?" To which one of my fellow explosive experts responded, "Oh, probably nothing more than make a loud noise." With that statement the die was cast!

In your wildest dreams you can't comprehend how many rocks, snakes, fish, snail darters, tree stumps, empty Coke bottles, discarded car tires, etc, etc, can be displaced by one small stick of dynamite. We also made another startling discovery—I don't know if you are aware—but did you know that it doesn't take much of an explosion to reroute the flow of a river?

We were all so surprised at the result that to this day none of us ever spoke of that incident again. For weeks all we heard from neighbors was their questioning each other if they heard that loud clap of thunder on the Fourth. It was the talk of the barbershop, the beauty salon, and all the usual gatherings at the local mercantile stores. The explosion was blamed on everything from sonic booms to flying saucers to old man Pogue's 10-gauge shotgun shooting at those dad-blasted hippie trespassers again. No one ever knew the source of the explosion except us, and we weren't telling! It always amazed me that none of our parents ever tied three revealing factors together. First, all us boys who participated in that dastardly deed couldn't hear very well for weeks.

Secondly, our wet clothes that were riddled with evidence testified that we had been either in or near the river. And third, no one ever questioned why there were dead fish floating in the river, coupled with a truckload of displaced rocks and stumps that littered Mr. Moore's soybean field.

Have you ever been in a situation where you were tempted to do something, but despite your best efforts to the contrary you gave in? Unfortunately, many Christians find themselves facing those types of temptations time and time again. To be honest there is no simple 1-2-3 formula for winning over temptation but there are some definite keys which will weaken its persistent attack. (1) Resolve to live your life in dependence upon God. (2) Make sure you choose wisely and weigh all the factors before you act. (3) Discipline yourself to have a pure heart and a strong will set on obedience to God. (4) Pick your friends wisely because failure to do so could cause you to blow it!

The Skillet Scandal

"A faithful witness will not lie: but a false witness
will utter lies."
Proverbs 14:5

Living in a small town like Lick Skillet had its advantages as well as disadvantages. One advantage was the sense of community where your neighbors looked out for each other's interests. If you happened to be out of town or away from home you could be assured that your property was being watched and protected by your neighbors. If both parents worked outside the home you would not have to worry about your kids coming home alone in the afternoons after school. Most kids would simply get off the bus at their neighbor's house and remain there until their parents came home from work.

The disadvantages were somewhat related to the advantages. Yes, you could go to your neighbor's house, but if you got into trouble while there the neighbor would discipline you just as severely as your parents. To make matters worse, once your parents came home from work the neighbor would tell them what you did which resulted in more punishment. It was hard for us kids living in the Skillet to get away with much because you had every adult in the entire community constantly watching your every move.

Another disadvantage of living in a small town is that everybody knows everyone else's business. It did not matter if you were an adult or a kid. If you did something you were not supposed to do it did not take long for the news to saturate the entire community. In the Skillet we had basically three modes of communication: telephone, telegraph and tell-it-to-your-neighbor. In my opinion, one of the dumbest inventions ever to befall humankind was the telephone company's old eight-party lines. Rarely could you use the telephone because you shared one line with seven other households. And believe me, every word that came out of your mouth made it to the ears of people who had nothing better to do than listen in on your conversations. There is no counting how many fights and fusses resulted between neighbors over the use of the telephone. PTA meetings at LSU (Lick Skillet University) were disrupted because the root cause was a dispute between neighbors over telephone use. Friendships were broken, churches split, and fences erected—all because of the eight-party line telephone system.

In most cases, by the time the news of some sordid event got to the local mercantile, the truth was frequently lost somewhere in translation as it passed from one mouth to the other. Usually, in more cases than not, what you ended up with was more of an exaggerated parody of the real thing.

Such was the case of a woman in our community whose reputation was sorely soiled by her momentary lapse in judgment. To understand what happened to her you must first appreciate how things were back in the 1950s and 60s. There was not very much traffic back then, other than an occasional farm tractor that would slowly limp past your house. About the greatest excitement of the day was the local mail delivery. For some reason going to the mailbox always gave adults a thrill and something to look forward to.

This is a really good indication that you need to get a life if the U.S. mail delivery is the most exciting event in your day. It was a hot summer day when this lady finished taking her daily bath. She had just slipped into her bathrobe when she noticed through the window the mailman making his daily delivery. Right away she became excited and couldn't wait to retrieve the surprises that might be lurking in that mailbox. Immediately she began devising a sneaky plan of attack on how she might get to that mail without putting on any clothes. She rationalized that she was home alone and it also appeared that no one else seemed to be around, so she could probably go out there without being seen.

There were several things wrong with her plan. One, the mailbox was a good 100 feet from the house to the road. Second, she still had on her bathrobe and nothing else. Third, the front yard has a few holes and uneven spots where moles and underground varmints made their home. And fourth, it is amazing how all these factors play into a great story...

According to reliable Lick Skillet sources, this lady embarked on her mission of retrieving her mail without getting dressed. She first peeped through the front door, looked left, then right to make sure no traffic was anywhere in sight. Then she reasoned that even if someone did see her they could not possibly know she didn't have anything on beneath her bathrobe. And third, on top of all these factors, she decided that if she ran fast enough she could pull this off (pun intended) and she would be back in a flash.

Plan in hand, she bolted out that door like a racehorse coming out of the starting gate during the Kentucky Derby, heading toward the mailbox. She made it just fine going; however, it was the return trip where she found herself in a bit of a dilemma. Just about halfway on her return trip, traveling at a high rate of speed across the yard, her right foot found one of those mole holes and set off a series of events that would forever change her life. She did a complete somersault which resulted in a face-first landing, culminating with a belly slide that would be the envy of any professional baseball player coming to home plate. Finally, her body stopped its forward motion but unfortunately the same could not be said of her bathrobe. See, long after her body had ground to a halt her bathrobe kept traveling which resulted in her bare essentials being completely exposed to the entire world.

Immediately the lady sprang to her feet and quickly looked around to see if anyone had witnessed this fiasco. She did not see anyone and breathed a sigh of relief, figuring that she had gotten away with an otherwise embarrassing moment. And it might have worked except for a few minor details. One, she did not realize until she got to her front porch that her neighbor was plowing his cotton field directly across from her house. Second, it just happened that he was at the point behind her mailbox where he got a full view. Third, the farmer served on the school board and was also known as the 'mouth of the south' around the Skillet. Putting all these factors together you have the makings of a real character assassination.

Which brings us to our words of wisdom for the day, "An hypocrite with his mouth destroyeth his neighbor; but through knowledge shall the just be delivered" (Proverbs 11:9).

If there is one thing all of us need it is a renewed sense of mutual respect and understanding for others. There is not a single one of us who does not have weaknesses and blind spots we are not aware of but of which are certainly apparent to others. This is why we need to make sure we do not capitalize on the weaknesses and mistakes of others to inflate our own egos or cover personal shortcomings. Integrity and personal character are precious personality traits that take years to establish. Unfortunately, it only takes one individual with a loose tongue and a few imagined facts to destroy in a moment what took years to establish.

Remember, it is true that we live in America where we have the tremendous benefit of freedom of speech. But freedom also carries with it personal responsibility for how we use or abuse the privilege. We are accountable to others for our words and deeds and will one day be ultimately accountable to God as well. Therefore, make absolutely sure it is not you that takes the tumble by failing to keep a guard on your tongue when speaking of others.

Tornadoes

"A wise man will hear, and will increase learning; and a man of understanding shall attain unto wise counsels."
Proverbs 1:5

Springtime in Lick Skillet always filled me with anticipation and excitement. The coldness and harshness of winter had passed and things like baseball, cutting grass, planting agricultural crops, and hanging out with my friends had finally arrived.

But for me, spring also brought a touch of mixed emotion because it also marked the beginning of tornado season.

When I was a growing up in rural Madison County, storms were a way of life, and I never gave them much thought. In my young mind, a mind totally oblivious to danger, when storms came I was always somewhat pleased because it meant no outside work like mowing grass or working in the fields. But on April 3, 1974, all that drastically changed. That was the day that our community found itself in the path of a series of deadly tornados that rocked and overwhelmed our community. Literally hundreds of tornadoes, one after another, sowed their devastation. Everyone was touched by the disasters in some way. In our little community every structure except the United Methodist Church and the small house behind it (where my wife and I happened to live) was destroyed. The landscape was rearranged and will never be the same again. Many or our friends and neighbors were either seriously injured or killed during these terrible and unusual phenomena.

Have you ever experienced a circumstance so horrific that it promotes a paralyzing realization of helplessness and fear? Or the power of a monster that has the potential to kill, maim, and destroy life and can literally forever change life as you know it?

I suppose all Americans experienced those feelings during the Oklahoma bombing and the World Trade Center attack as we watched the families of those killed searching for their relatives.

Watching people's lives radically change because of circumstances beyond their control is a devastating thing. It does not leave us with memories that are readily forgotten, nor do the emotional scars heal easily.

All of us experience circumstances that contain the potential of dragging us down and hindering God's will of joy, contentment, and peace. I believe the devil is good at taking our past bad experiences and using them against us. People often cannot or will not accept Jesus Christ as their personal Lord and Savior because they think they are not good enough. Others who have done things that they are ashamed of convince themselves that God "couldn't possibly love or use someone like me." Time after time I've counseled with people who have failures in their past (some of their own making and others who are victims of circumstances beyond their control) that they just cannot seem to get beyond. Their life could be compared to an old phonograph record that keeps repeating the same lyrics over and over again because the needle can't get past the defect.

Don't allow your circumstances, the world, the devil, or others to dictate who you are! If you know Jesus Christ as your Savior, you are a child of the King and you need to hold your head high and act like a member of the royal family. We are kingdom people! We need to advance in the name of the Lord and allow Him to use our failures as steppingstones to victory. Like that giant tornado of '74, the devil is nothing more than a big windbag anyway! God made sure of that when He took the wind out of his sails at the resurrection of Jesus Christ.

Joyride Gone Bad

"The wise shall inherit glory: but shame shall be the promotion of fools."
Proverbs 3:35

Growing up as a typical teenager in Lick Skillet during late 60s and 70s had its interesting moments. Like most young people of that era, we were no different from any other teens living in American cities, suburbs, and rural areas. I'm sure young people living in North Alabama did their fair share of protesting the Vietnam war, burning their draft cards, hating Lyndon Johnson, and watching *Laugh In* and *Hee Haw* on television.

For me it was no different. I lapsed into that period of life when most parents swear their kids have lost all semblance of sanity. You remember? Those days when we walked around in a stupor with a blank stare on our face, not knowing if we were here or there? And in the 60s and 70s we dressed in strange garb. Our pant legs looked like the Liberty Bell without the crack. To help us keep our pants on we wore wide belts with words like *peace* and *groovy* inscribed on the leather. We sported bright multi-colored shirts with wild stripes and wore funky-looking floppy hats with flowers stuck in them. And we sang dumb songs with lyrics like, "there she was just a settin' next to me, singing do-wa-diddy-diddy-dum-diddy-do!"

There was one incident that occurred in the summer of 1968 that just adds to the insanity of the era. My buddies and I had just turned sixteen years of age and all of us had just gotten our driver's licenses. On that Sunday afternoon several of us decided to go joy riding in my best friend's 1953 Ford custom automobile. You talk about an immaculate car! He washed and waxed and shined that thing until the paint wore off. On this day, as we six amigos were traveling along, one of our companions decided that it would be fun to throw an M-80 firework out the window of our moving car. There were just two things wrong with this idea. One, the guy doing the throwing was sitting in the back seat between two other geniuses. Two, the one doing the throwing didn't realize it, but my friend who owned the car had just spent his entire Saturday really, really, *really* cleaning his windows.

Let's take a deep breath: an M-80 is equivalent to a quarter stick of dynamite and can cause lots of damage and make a really, really, *really* huge noise. I'm here to testify that you haven't lived until you see a guy light the fuse on an M-80 and sling it against a very clean automobile window that is up. The last thing I heard (for several days) was someone yelling, "Oh no! Everybody duck-k-k-k!!" Then came that tremendous B-O-O-O-M! The next thing I remember was all of those used-to-be-clean windows coming down and six hippie wannabes hanging out of that '53 Ford doing 60 mph with blue and white gunpowder smoke billowing out of every crack and crevice. Bell-bottom pants legs clanged, flowery shirts wilted, and we all walked around for days singing, "do-wa-diddy-diddy-dum-diddy-do!"

I learned quite a lot that day. I learned that overlooking details and making wrong assumptions can get you into lots of trouble. And it is bad enough when those assumptions pertain to this life, but it is a spiritual disaster when it applies to eternity. The apostle Paul said, "They profess that they know God; but in works they deny him, being abominable, and disobedient, and unto every good work reprobate" (Titus 1:16). Paul makes it absolutely clear that making the wrong assumptions can and will have disastrous results.

Don't throw away your Christian testimony and good name by being stupid and acting like a jerk. Unfortunately, many Christians have the same attitude about their spirituality as my friend with the M-80. They are careless, reckless, and self-centered. I agree with the old adage that says, "If you're going to be stupid you've got to be tough!"

Don't Lose Your Hunker

"Be careful for nothing; but in every thing by prayer and
supplication with thanksgiving let your requests
be made known unto God."
Philippians 4:6

While growing up in the Skillet, church attendance in
the Fanning household was not only a way of life it
was also a requirement. I have to admit that attending
church, along with all my other required attendee friends,
was not my most joyous priority for the weekend. Most of
the church buildings were not air-conditioned, which meant
that in the spring and summer the congregation had all the
windows opened so they could catch an occasional breeze
while listening to our pastor fray away at his hour-long
sermon on sin. My Methodist buddies were fortunate
enough to live in the richer section (which meant they had
two-holer outhouses instead of one) of town because at least
they had window fans to keep them comfortable, which, by
the way, was a source of controversy between the two
denominations. The Baptists accused the Methodists of
wasting God's money on foolish and self-centered things
such as window fans. Baptists, until a few years ago, had a

problem with being relaxed in church and stood on their theological conviction that everybody must suffer and be uncomfortable to be spiritual. Today, if the air-conditioning isn't right, the pews padded, and sermon short we think we have been unduly persecuted for righteousness' sake.

Back then, our church had its share of good, godly people who loved Jesus and served Him to the best of their ability. There was one elderly man within the congregation whom our pastor would occasionally call upon to lead in public prayer, usually just prior to taking the morning offering. Whenever this man would pray all us boys would look at each other and grin because we all knew what was about to happen. To him, prayer was an exercise and he appeared to us to be preparing more for a foot race than leading in prayer. Without fail, every time he would rise to his feet, move out into the aisle, momentarily hesitate, then begin to slightly bounce up and down on the balls of his feet, shake his arms, roll his head and rub his neck, all for the purpose of generally preparing himself for the task at hand. He then would pinch the material of his trousers just above the knee and pull them up slightly so as not to bind himself when he knelt to pray. Then he would position himself in a squatting position in the middle of the aisle, place his elbow on his knee, and gently rest his forehead in a bowed posture.

One Sunday evening our pastor called upon this dear man to lead in prayer. Immediately he began his usual ritual and after a time of preparation he was finally in his bowed position. But this time, as he intently got into the meat of his praying, his elbow slipped off his knee causing him to lose his balance, thereby resulting in him rolling, spread-eagled, to the floor. No matter, the man never uttered a word or grunted amongst the stifled laughter and sniggering in the congregation (boys, girls, men, and women were trying not to laugh, even the pastor let a small smile slip). Undaunted, the man merely got to his feet, went through his preparatory routine again, got back in his usual position, and humbly and simply resumed his prayer by saying, "Lord, forgive me! I just temporarily lost my hunker!"

As I think of this amusing story, I must admit that this poor man probably taught more correct theology than he realized. He may have had a rather unique way of saying it, but the fact is, when we are prayerless, everything spirals out of balance and we end up losing something very significant. One of my favorite passages of Scripture says, *"Call unto me, and I will answer thee, and shew thee great and mighty things, which thou knowest not"* (Jeremiah 33:3).

Here, God is speaking through the great prophet, exhorting His people to prayer. God yearns to show His people things of the Spirit that we can never know any way apart from consistent communication with Him.

Let me encourage you to make prayer to God an important part of your day. Remember: failure to persevere in prayer may cost us more than merely the loss of our hunker!

"Preach It, Brother!"

"Through desire a man, having separated himself, seeketh
and intermeddleth with all wisdom."
Proverbs 18:1

Several years ago I was invited to preach in an African-
American church. It was an eventful evening and my
wife and I enjoyed every moment. Preaching to an African-
American congregation and attempting to adapt to their
style of worship is a unique experience. The atmosphere is
exciting and celebrative and the congregation actually talks
back to you during the sermon. Unlike their white counterparts who mainly just sit and listen as you preach, the
African-American congregations actually help you preach.
The entire congregation literally becomes involved in the
sermon delivery and if you are not careful you will get
caught up and simply lose yourself in the exciting atmosphere. My wife laughed at me because when I would say
something the people considered good they would yell,
"Preach it, brother!" Or, "Say it again." So I naturally would
say it again! Later my wife said, "I don't think they really
meant for you to actually say it again!" Those dear people
nearly preached me to death and before I got off that

platform I appeared as though I had just run a marathon.

I also discovered something else about the African-American church. I was told that it is customary for the host pastor to be responsible for the introduction of the guest speaker, as well as to say a prayer of blessing just prior to the sermon. These prayers are directed to the throne of God, requesting His power to fall on the speaker as well as those who will be listening. Many times the senior pastor's prayers are more powerful than the actual sermon.

Take for example this prayer that I found many years ago that was written by an unknown author as he quoted an elderly senior pastor just prior to a guest speaker....

O Lord, give thy servant this evening the eyes of the eagle and the wisdom of the owl. Connect his soul with the gospel telephone of that great central station in the skies. Luminate his brow with the sunshine of heaven and pizen his mind with the love for the people. Turpentine his imagination and don't forget to grease his lips with possum oil. Loosen his tongue with the sledgehammer of thy power. Lectify his brain with the lightning of thy Word. Put 'pectual motion in his arms so he can frail away at the onslaughts of the devil that's sure to get in his face. Fill him plum full of the dynamite of thy glory and 'noint him all over with the verssine oil of thy salvation. And we'd be remiss if we didn't ask that you set him ablaze with the gospel fires so he can burn, burn, burn. So let him burn, Lord, let him burn! And we ask this all for Jesus' sake, amen!

Unique, but pointed, would you not agree? It doesn't matter how you say it, prayer is an indispensable part of the Christian life and without it we are a powerless people. Prayer is the necessary ingredient that turns a gathering into a worship service. It is the source that transforms a song from mere entertainment into praise and adoration. Prayer is the power that will convert a speech to a sermon. Prayer will change your meager existence into an exciting, Spirit-filled life. We all need to understand that in this life we are not fighting a physical battle. The war we wage is for the minds and souls of people. Therefore, the way we do battle is different. Prayer is by far more powerful than any man-made bomb when it comes to a battle of a spiritual nature. Satan is not a powerless foe because he has strong ways to try and capture the minds and hearts of people. It is incumbent upon all of us to allow Jesus Christ to capture our thinking so we do not fall victim to Satan's devices. We must nourish our relationship with Christ through prayer every day and absorb as much spiritual information as we can to help offset the harmful, fiery darts that are cast our way. Like the old pastor's prayer, *"Set our hearts ablaze with the gospel fires so we can burn, burn, burn."*

King of the Hill

"An evil man seeketh only rebellion: therefore a cruel
messenger shall be sent against him."
Proverbs 17:11

I suppose every town and most every school has its bully.
You know, the one who thinks he is the meanest, toughest
guy on the block. Bullies always make it their business to
whip up on somebody else (usually someone who is much
smaller and weaker than himself) just to let everybody know
who is the king of the hill. If there is trouble anywhere, a
fight at a high school ballgame, problems at the school
dance, community activity, sporting event—whatever and
wherever—this person is usually in the middle of it.

The majority of us country farm boys who grew up in
the Skillet were polite Southern gentlemen who used
expressions like "yes um" when asked a question by the
teacher in class. Or "naw sir" when confronted by the principal. If you met someone in the hall the usual greeting was
"Howdy." If it happened to be a group of people you would
say, "Howdy, ya'll." And if you were really interested in the
person or wanted to inquire about their family you would
say, "How's ye mama and nim doin'?" Most of the time we

didn't actually care to know how *mamma and nim* were doing; it was just polite to ask. It never failed that there would always be that exceptional case that took your inquiry seriously and would begin telling you how mamma and nim, daddy and nim, and just plain everybody and nim were getting along. But most folks just minded their own business and kept their nose where it belonged.

But there was this one guy who will remain anonymous due to health reasons (mine!) who did a masterful job of kicking other people's derrière. For him, inflicting bodily harm on his neighbors and nim was an art form. He learned early how to start at the knees and gradually move up the body toward your head. Then he would make sure all the scratches and scrapes ran in the same direction like the grain on an oak board. He knew just how hard to hit so that all the bruises would have the same discoloration (usually light black, highlighted with pale blue with just a tad of yellow). He viewed his ability to accomplish this as his special trademark. He got the idea from watching a Zorro movie where old Zorro would leave his famous Z after he had just made short order out of the bad guys. If you happened to see someone the next day who had the misfortune to encounter bully boy, you wouldn't need to ask who he tangled with. You would just know by the famous discolored trademark on his face and the direction of his scrapes and scratches. Believe me, an encounter with our bully friend was something you wanted to avoid at all costs.

That is until the day that bully boy met Cochise (his nickname). Cochise was a little wiry, full-blooded American Indian who may have weighed 110 pounds soaking wet. He had long flowing coal-black hair and wore a red bandana to keep the hair out of his eyes. He was a quiet boy with a shy personality and certainly lacked any social skills. He mainly kept to himself and did not bother anybody. He would speak when spoken to, but was somewhat of a mystery because no one ever got to be close friends with him. His parents had moved to North Alabama from South Dakota seeking work in the local chicken houses. There were several members of his family who all worked hard but generally isolated themselves from the rest of the community. One Saturday afternoon bully boy spotted Cochise sitting in his automobile at a convenience store parking lot in downtown Skillet. Immediately bully boy was inspired by an overwhelming wave of intelligence and decided that he wanted to drive little Cochise's car. After repeating his sarcastic request to let him behind the steering wheel, coupled with Cochise' non-responsive attitude, bully boy walked over and grabbed that little Indian by the collar and commenced to drag him across the seat and out the passenger side of that automobile.

Have you ever heard a bobcat scream? If you haven't, it sounds like a cross between an upset chimpanzee and a hysterical woman who has just seen a rat. For me, that was just about what the noise coming from bully boy sounded like once that little Indian was out of that car and on his feet. He took hold of bully boy's throat, and I'm not certain, but I would have bet a dollar that bully boy temporarily thought he had just met Cochise and nim instead of just one little Indian boy!

It didn't take Cochise but a moment to demonstrate that he was a better derrière-kicking artist than bully boy and it was surely evident to all of us that Cochise had majored in derrière rearrangement before moving to Alabama.

When the fight was over, our bully friend couldn't figure out where his nose and ears were supposed to be. He spent the next two weeks sipping soup though a straw and trying to make out some semblance of daylight through his swollen, squinted eyes.

You know something? Bully boy reminds me of Satan and how he operates in the lives of all people. The apostle

Peter says, "Be sober, be vigilant; because your adversary the devil, as a roaring lion, walketh about, seeking whom he may devour" (1 Peter 5:8). Later the apostle Paul would warn, "Put on the whole armour of God, that ye may be able to stand against the wiles of the devil" (Ephesians 6:11).

The devil may be a master at the art of intimidation, violence, and death, but the fact is there was another young man with long flowing hair who also proved to be superior. Jesus Christ came to earth in the form of a man, picked up a cross, and marched to the top of Calvary's mount. Once there, He established forever who was King of the hill!

With love for us all, Jesus put a stop to Satan dragging God's people across the seat of life. Jesus, by His sacrifice on the cross and His glorious resurrection from the dead made a public spectacle of Satan and proved he is nothing more than mere hot air and a great big windbag.

Isn't it interesting that it took a meek, humble little American Indian to show us the truth about our own Lick Skillet bully? But isn't it much greater that a meek, humble Jewish carpenter revealed the truth about the bully of all our souls, Satan? What about you? Has Satan been dragging you across the seat of life lately?

Printed in the United States
34572LVS00003B/82-1008